# SPIRITUAL
## Warfare

# Discovery House Publishers

*Books, music, and videos that feed the soul with the Word of God*

Box 3566 Grand Rapids, MI 49501

Winning the daily battle with Satan

RAY C. STEDMAN

Discovery House Publishers is affiliated with RBC Ministries,
Grand Rapids, Michigan 49512

Discovery House books are distributed to the trade exclusively by
Barbour Publishing, Inc., Uhrichsville, Ohio 44683

**Library of Congress Cataloging-in-Publication Data**

Stedman, Ray C.
  Spiritual warfare / by Ray C. Stedman
        p.    cm.
  Originally published: Waco, Tex. : Word Books, 1975, in series:
     Discovery books.
  ISBN 1-57293-044-6
  1. Spiritual warfare.  2. Christian life.  I. Title.
  BV4501.2.S739  1999
  248.4—dc21                                              98-54138
                                                              CIP

*Printed in the United States of America*

01 03 04 05 02
CHG
5 7 9 10 8 6 4

# Contents

# The Battle is the Lord's

IT WAS A WARM, QUIET SUNDAY MORNING on the Hawaiian island of Oahu. The date was December 7, 1941. Out of a clear blue sky, swarms of growling aircraft descended. Suddenly, all around Pearl Harbor, ships erupted into flames and billows of oily black smoke. Within those ships, men died without a moment's warning—some even asleep in their bunks.

Aboard the cruiser *New Orleans*, a chaplain named Howell M. Forgy helped a group of crewmen break into a locked ammunition storeroom so the ship could mount a defense. Once Chaplain Forgy and the other men got inside, they discovered that the ammunition hoist was out of commission. So Chaplain Forgy and the other men formed a human chain, like a bucket brigade, passing the heavy artillery shells from man to man up to the gun deck.

The shells were heavy and the work was hard and discouraging, and it had to be carried on amid the smell of smoke and the sound of human screams and roaring planes and exploding bombs. Chaplain Forgy saw that some of the men's arms were weakening and their faces showed signs of hopelessness. So he pasted a broad smile on his face, slapped the back of the man next to him, and shouted, "Praise the Lord and pass the ammunition!"

This story was later retold, and the chaplain's words became the opening lines of a popular wartime song that lifted the spirits of an entire nation at war.

You and I face much the same situation today. We are under heavy attack—a spiritual and moral attack—and the devastation of this spiritual war is all around us in our society, our government, our universities, our entertainment media, our neighborhoods, our families, our churches, and our own lives. There are wounded people all around us, and we ourselves have been pierced by the fiery arrows of our enemy. To survive and to win, we must mount a strong defense and engage the enemy in battle. We must learn to "praise the Lord—and pass the ammunition!"

And who is this enemy who is trying to destroy us?

Behind the confusion and fog of the battle is a crafty, powerful, and devastatingly real spiritual being whom our Lord Jesus has called "the ruler of this world," the devil. Despite the current surge of interest in the occult, New Age beliefs, and satanism, there is still a shocking ignorance on the part of Christians everywhere as to how to deal with the devil and his schemes.

It is time we who believe in the Lord Jesus Christ accept the fact that life is warfare, and that we are engaged in a life-and-death struggle. The forces we face are not flesh-and-blood enemies, nor are they human agencies. But they are as real as any enemy who ever wielded a sword, a gun, or a flame-thrower. Our enemy is legion—a deadly pantheon of spiritual hosts of wickedness. Though invisible, these forces are utterly dedicated to our destruction.

These forces operate under the authority of the one who is the father of lies, the prince of darkness, the devil himself. Only by recognizing him as real, as the Scriptures clearly declare, can we begin to understand the reality around us. Only then can we truly live life as it really is. Only then can we comprehend the vital necessity of putting on the whole armor of God which, far from being merely a figure of speech, is in fact Christ Himself.

In our own strength we are utterly helpless to face such a powerful enemy as the devil. In fact, true victory in spiritual warfare demands that we acknowledge our helplessness and weakness. God has given us three specific steps that enable us to be conquerors:

First, we are to lay hold of the complete protection of Christ, what the Bible calls the full armor of God.

Second, once fully armed, we are to pray. Effective prayer is the result of actively putting on the armor of God.

Third and finally, in the face of Satan's attacks, we are to stand firm in our faith with the certain knowledge that the battle is the Lord's. Our faith in His victory—a victory that is already accomplished on the cross—is what overcomes the world.

The purpose of this book to help you where help is most needed: in the day-to-day conflict where our enemy continually attacks us in the form of open hostilities, subtle temptations, festering worries and resentments, gnawing fears, bitter disappointments, and that vague and nameless depression of spirit that so often attacks us and robs us of peace and sleep at 3:00 o'clock in the morning. Here is where the great spiritual issues are really won or lost—and where the great resources of Christ are more needed than at any other time.

Ray C. Stedman

Author's Note: I gladly acknowledge my great debt to the fine series of studies by Dr. Martyn Lloyd-Jones on Ephesians 6, published serially in *The Westminster Record*; and to the pastoral staff of Peninsula Bible Church for their unfailing encouragement.

*Finally, be strong in the Lord and in his mighty power. Put on the full armor of God so that you can take your stand against the devil's schemes. For our struggle is not against flesh and blood, but against the rulers, against the authorities, against the powers of this dark world and against the spiritual forces of evil in the heavenly realms. Therefore put on the full armor of God, so that when the day of evil comes, you may be able to stand your ground, and after you have done everything, to stand.*

**Ephesians 6:10–13**

# 1

# The Forces We Face

GOD IS NOT INTERESTED IN RELIGION, but He is tremendously interested in life. You cannot read the New Testament without realizing that the Lord Jesus did not hesitate to break the Sabbath regulations of His day when those regulations violated the real need of a broken human being for healing. God is not nearly so interested in stained-glass windows, organ music, congregational hymns, or pastoral prayers as He is in producing love-filled homes, generous hearts, and brave men and women who can live godly lives in the midst of a dark and evil world. His goal for our lives is that we be people of undefiled minds and undefiled hearts, living and projecting His truth and His character in a sin-ridden world.

I am deeply convinced that we can only understand life when we see it as the Bible sees it. That is why the Word of God was given—to open our eyes to God's perspective on life and reality. The world we see all around us—the world of entertainment and nightly news and instant information on the Internet and political infighting and social upheaval—that is a world of illusion. Though we usually call it "the real world," it is a façade that is destined to fade away. What God calls reality is something that exists beyond the flimsy walls of this world, and it is far more real and lasting than our so-called "real world." Our eyes and minds are constantly deceived by the distorted perspectives, twisted beliefs, false values, and temporary programs of this dying world.

But when we come to the Bible, we learn the truth. Here reality is laid before us, and we see the world as it really is. When we get down to the bare essentials of life and strip off all the confusing illusion, we find that life is exactly what the Bible records it to be.

We may not want to hear what the Bible has to say to us. We may think the Bible's diagnosis of our condition is too harsh, or its prescription for our healing is too difficult—but if we reject its truth, we only succeed in deceiving ourselves. We would prefer to "cherry-pick" God's truth—to highlight the verses we like and edit out the verses that expose our sins and failures. But it is not up to us to pass judgment on God's Word. Rather, we must submit ourselves to the judgment of God's Word, because it is inspired by God Himself. We do not have the authority to "correct" His words; rather, those words are the authority that correct our lives.

So let's stop this silly business of sitting in judgment upon the insights of the Lord Jesus Christ. In this world, we are continually confronted with the choice of whether to accept the flimsy, fallible "authority" of mere human beings or the certain, unfailing, clear Word of the Lord

Jesus Christ. But as Christians, as people who bear the name of Christ, we must continually reduce every argument to this simple consideration: "Am I to accept this person's word—or the Word of Christ? If this person's word agrees with what the Lord says, then fine, it is truth. But if this person's word does not agree with God's Word, then I must reject it, because there is no authority greater than that of God."

## Life is struggle

In Ephesians 6, the apostle Paul sets forth his analysis of life, especially as it relates to the Christian life. And in Paul's analysis, life is struggle, life is conflict, life is warfare. Under the inspiration of God, Paul writes:

> Finally, be strong in the Lord and in his mighty power. Put on the full armor of God so that you can take your stand against the devil's schemes. For our struggle is not against flesh and blood, but against the rulers, against the authorities, against the powers of this dark world and against the spiritual forces of evil in the heavenly realms. Therefore put on the full armor of God, so that when the day of evil comes, you may be able to stand your ground, and after you have done everything, to stand. (Ephesians 6:10–13)

Nowhere in this passage do you get any sense that (as an old popular song used to put it) "life is just a bowl of cherries." No, stripped to its essentials, life is nothing more or less than a long struggle, a never-ending wrestling match. We don't like this idea, of course. We feel entitled to a life that is essentially care-free and easy, with just enough work to do to keep us busy and interested. We feel we have a right to expect the kind of life described in another old popular song:

> We'll build a sweet little nest,
> Somewhere in the West,
> And let the rest of the world go by.

We tend to think of the trials, pressures, and problems of life as an annoying and unfair intrusion into our rightful, neat, and orderly existence. But Paul says that those afflictions and problems are not *intrusions* into our lives— *they are life itself!* They are the stuff of which life is made— conflict, struggle, and difficult choices.

Now, there's nothing wrong with dreaming dreams and making plans for the future. There is nothing wrong with enjoying life. In fact, our romantic and idealized dreams of "the good life" are a kind of racial memory, the vestigial remains of what was once God's intention for men and women. In God's good order and time, the golden age we all long for will become a reality—but it will take place in the life to come, not in the life of the here and now.

The apostle Paul tells us that life is a struggle, a life- and-death conflict between two opposing forces. If we try to ignore the conflict, if we do not firmly choose the right side and take up our armor and our weapons for the battle, we will inevitably find ourselves jarred and shaken by spiritual reality. We may even become casualties of a battle we thought we could wish away. Truth has a way of intruding on our pleasant little illusions.

We all know what it's like to have to shed our illusions and face the truth. The vacation ends, and we must leave Disneyland or Tahiti or Paris and return to the everyday world of making a living. Or a loved one dies, and we must face loneliness, grief, and the utterly real fact of human mortality. Or we lose our health. Or we lose our prosperity. Or we suffer some other personal loss. It happens all the time. We are continually shaken out of our dreams and daydreams, and we are forced to face the hard realities of life and eternity.

In *Proceedings*, the magazine of the Naval Institute, naval officer Frank Koch tells the story of an incident that happened to him at sea—an incident that illustrates the principle Paul talks about:

Two battleships assigned to the training squadron had been at sea on maneuvers in heavy weather for several days. I was serving on the lead battleship and was on watch on the bridge as night fell. The visibility was poor with patchy fog, so the captain remained on the bridge keeping an eye on all activities.

Shortly after dark, the lookout on the wing of the bridge reported, "Light, bearing on the starboard bow."

"Is it steady or moving astern?" the captain called out.

Lookout replied, "Steady, captain," which meant we were on a dangerous collision course with that ship.

The captain then called to the signalman, "Signal that ship: We are on a collision course, advise you change course 20 degrees."

Back came a signal, "Advisable for you to change course 20 degrees."

The captain said, "Send, I'm a captain, change course 20 degrees."

"I'm a petty officer second class," came the reply. "You had better change course 20 degrees."

By that time, the captain was furious. He spat out, "Send, I'm a battleship. Change course 20 degrees."

Back came the flashing light, "I'm a lighthouse."

We changed course.

God's truth is like that lighthouse—and we are like that battleship. In our human arrogance, we chart our own course and demand that the world adjust itself to our wishes. But God's truth is unchanging, unbending, unyielding. It is not God's duty to alter His truth. It is our responsibility to chart our course according to the light of His Word, which is ultimate, objective reality. If we fail to do so, we risk running our lives aground.

## "When the day of evil comes . . ."

The apostle Paul says that this struggle we face varies in intensity from one day to the next. We must learn to stand, he says, "when the day of evil comes." This implies that not all days are evil. Some days will be worse than others. There are seasons in our lives when pressures are more intense, and when problems, trials, and temptations seem to gang up on us all at once. These are what we recognize as evil days. The "day of evil" may not be a literal twenty-four-hour day, of course—it could be a day, a week, or even years in length. But thank God, all of life is not a relentless, excruciating trial. There are certainly times in life when we get a rest from the battle, a reduction of the pressure, a relief from overpowering circumstances and agonizing decisions.

The reason we are not always under pressure is because of the grace of God. The fact is that all of life truly would be a day of evil—and much worse!—if not for the grace and goodness of a loving God. He continually operates to restrain the powers that war against us and to allow times of refreshment, recreation, enjoyment, and blessing. It is tragic that we so often take these times of refreshment for granted, enjoying them without a single thought for the goodness of God which makes them possible. Instead of giving thanks to God for those times of refreshment, we feel entitled to God's blessing, and we are quick to complain that God is unfair when life doesn't go according to our expectations. This is the point Paul makes in his letter to the Romans:

> Or do you show contempt for the riches of his kindness, tolerance and patience, not realizing that God's kindness leads you toward repentance? (Romans 2:4).

So while every day is not an evil day, we have to agree with God's Word when it tells us that, in general, life is an unrelenting struggle. The struggle varies in intensity from time to time, but it extends from the cradle to the grave.

## The nature of our struggle

Paul then goes on to analyze and define for us the nature of the struggle—and this is a crucial point to understand. He tells us that our conflict is not against flesh and blood. That is, spiritual warfare is not about the struggle of man against man. It is not a political struggle, a social struggle, an economic struggle, or even a religious-theological-doctrinal struggle. It is not a struggle *between* human beings. It is a struggle *within* human beings.

Let me ask you a question: What is the one thing that gives you the most difficulty in life? For most of us, the answer to that question, in one form or another, comes down to one thing: People. You may struggle intensely with a family member, your spouse or child or a parent. Or you may have personality conflicts and struggles in your office, or in your church, or in your neighborhood.

In the political realm, the Republicans are always vexed by the stratagems of the Democrats, and the Democrats are always irritated by the tactics of the Republicans—and both parties are annoyed with the Libertarians, Reform Party, Greens, and independents!

And let us not forget the Internal Revenue Service. Certainly if there is one group of people who know how to make our lives miserable, it is those "public servants" down at the IRS!

But the apostle Paul says that our struggle is not against flesh and blood. Our true battle is not against our political opponents or the IRS or family or co-workers or neighbors or any other human agency. The battle is not against people, but against unseen spiritual powers. In fact, the entire human race is under a vicious assault by certain principalities and powers, world rulers of darkness, wicked spirits in high places.

"That is your problem," Paul says, in effect. "That is the nature of the enemy we face—powerful invisible rulers of darkness, highly placed agents of spiritual wickedness!" And it is not just Christians who are opposed by these forces. Every man, every woman, every child, everywhere is a target of the enemy. The devil has each one of us in his crosshairs. The whole race is opposed by the principalities and powers, the world rulers of this present darkness. That is Paul's explanation of the struggle of life.

Yet, even though the devil has declared war on the entire human race, it is only Christians who are capable of believing and perceiving the true nature of this conflict. The world does not understand spiritual truth, so it either distorts the true nature of our battle to the point of ridiculousness or it rejects spiritual reality as a "myth," intellectually unacceptable and inadmissible to any intelligent mind. Occultism and superstition have distorted the great revelation of spiritual warfare—the dark powers, rulers, authorities, and spiritual forces of evil in the heavenly realms—and have reduced them to a ridiculous pantheon of comic-book goblins, witches, spooks, and ghouls.

I am well aware of the disdain that many people in our society today exhibit toward any serious discussion of the devil and evil spiritual forces. They say, "Are you going to insult our intelligence by talking about a personal devil? That is such a medieval concept—straight out of the superstition of the Dark Ages! Are you seriously suggesting that the devil is at the root of all the world's problems today?" I have even encountered this attitude within the Christian church.

I once spent an evening in Berlin discussing these issues with four or five intelligent churchmen—men who knew the Bible intimately, from cover to cover. Though we never once opened a Bible, we spent the whole evening together discussing various passages. I never referred to a single passage of Scripture that these men were not aware of. In fact, they could quote these passages verbatim. Yet each of these churchmen rejected the idea of a personal devil. At the end of evening they admitted that, having rejected belief in the existence of the devil, they had no answers to the most puzzling issues of life, such as the obvious prevalence of evil in our world. We had to leave it there.

We have to ask ourselves, if there is no devil, then how do we explain all the evil in the world? When we look at the many attempts down through history to destroy God's chosen nation, Israel, including the Holocaust just a short half-century ago, how can we say there is no devil? How can we say that a personal, intentional force for evil is not deliberately trying to destroy God's plan for the world? And when we look at the persecution of the Christian church around the globe, God chosen agency for demonstrating His character and His love in a dark world, how can we say there is no devil?

The devil is real, he is active, he is working day and night, trying to subvert and undo and defeat God's plan in human history. The devil is our enemy.

And this is war.

## The desperate disease

Once we see reality as God sees it, through the lens of His Word, the Bible, we see that we must accept as fact the proposition of Paul in Ephesians 6: Behind the problems of the world, behind the evil that manifests itself in mankind, there is a hierarchy of evil spirits—the devil and his angels. The world says to the Christian, "Why talk about myths from the Bible about devils and angels? You want to know what's real? Turn on CNN or pick up the *Wall Street Journal* or the *Washington Post*—that's reality. That's relevant. That's meaningful."

No, that's ephemeral, that's passing away, that's the illusion of reality. *Real* reality, the real warfare that's going on in this world, is so invisible to the people of this world that it's never talked about on CNN, and it never makes the headlines—yet it is actually these principalities and powers that drive the events behind the headlines! The wars, the genocides, the persecutions, the famines, the hatred, the racial unrest—all of these things are the outward symptoms of the spiritual cancer that is consuming this world from the inside out.

And what good is it to keep giving aspirins to a feverish patient when the fever is merely a symptom of a deadly cancer? It is not enough to treat the symptoms—we must attack the disease itself. That is what Paul so vividly and accurately sets before us in Ephesians 6.

This crippling disease has reached such a deadly, critical stage that even worldlings, non-Christians, are recognizing the inadequacy of their diagnosis. Listen to Carl Jung, the great Swiss psychologist and medical doctor:

> We stand perplexed and stupefied before the phenomena of Marxism and Bolshevism because *we know nothing about man* or, at any rate, have only a lopsided

and distorted picture of him. If we had self-knowledge, that would not be the case. We stand face-to-face with the terrible question of evil and do not even know what is before us, let alone know what to pit against it. And even if we did know, we still cannot understand how it can happen here.

What a tremendously candid admission of human ignorance in the face of life as it really is! And listen to this bewildered cry from U Thant, when he was Secretary General of the United Nations. Speaking out on behalf of the dream of world peace before a conference of international delegates, he asked a question that is humanly unanswerable—but which God has already answered in His Word:

> What element is lacking so that with all our skill and all our knowledge we still find ourselves in the dark valley of discord and enmity? What is it that inhibits us from going forward together to enjoy the fruits of human endeavor and to reap the harvest of human experience? Why is it that, for all our professed ideals, our hopes, and our skills, peace on earth is still a distant objective seen only dimly through the storms and turmoils of our present difficulties?

As the world's great leaders grapple with the dilemma of modern life, all they can say is, "What is wrong? What is the unknown element behind this? We cannot understand or explain this! Something is missing from our understanding of human nature and human behavior. What is it?"

The answer: There is a spiritual war going on behind the scenes of history, and that spiritual war in the unseen world is driving events in our own visible world. There is no peace in the material world because there is a war now raging in the spiritual world.

There is nothing more meaningful, more relevant, more real that we could be involved in than the cause of God in this vast spiritual war. The biblical teaching of spiritual warfare shines a spotlight of truth on the basic problem of human existence and human history.

## From Genesis to Revelation

While modern sociology, psychology, and political science stand baffled and frustrated in the face of the world's evil and darkness, the apostle Paul gives us the insight and illumination of God's Word: The world, he says, is in the grip of what he calls "rulers . . . authorities . . . powers."

These rulers and powers of this dark world are headed by the devil, whom Scripture says is a fallen angel of malevolent power and cunning intelligence. It is the devil against whom Christians are called to wrestle daily. Now, that is not just the claim of one isolated passage of the Bible. That is the teaching of the Bible from beginning to end, from Genesis to Revelation, and especially *in* both Genesis and Revelation.

The Lord Jesus Himself put His finger on the whole problem when He said to certain men of His day, "You belong to your father, the devil, and you want to carry out your father's desire. He was a murderer from the beginning, not holding to the truth, for there is no truth in him. When he lies, he speaks his native language, for he is a liar and the father of lies" (John 8:44).

In that stark and startling analysis, the Lord stripped the devil of his disguises and revealed his true character—a liar and a murderer. What the devil does is related to what he is, just as what we do is precisely the result of what we are. Because he is a liar and a murderer, the devil's work is to deceive and to destroy. There you have the explanation for all the misery, hatred, murder, war, and other evils that have taken place in human history.

The devil has the ear of humankind. Scripture calls him "the god of this world." The world listens to him and to everything he says, but the devil does not tell the world the truth. The devil is a master of psychology, and he understands that people would much rather believe a pleasant, attractive lie than the unvarnished truth. That is why so many people rush to their destruction, ignoring all the evidence around them. They drool with desire after the attractive lies of the devil while rejecting the clear, life-giving truth of God.

Too late, people who chase the devil's lies discover that at the end of the lie is destruction and death—either a living death of shame, regret, self-hate, frustration, meaninglessness, and emptiness, or a literal physical death and a literal spiritual death in eternity. Whom the devil cannot deceive, he tries to destroy, and whom he cannot destroy, he attempts to deceive. That is the working of the devil.

### The call to arms

"Well," you say, "this is all very depressing. I would rather not think about it." I don't like to think about it either, but I have discovered that you cannot wish the truth away. There is only one realistic approach to this struggle, and that is to be strong in the Lord and in the power of his might. That is the way of escape, and there is no other.

God has issued to each of us a bugle call to intelligent combat. It is a call to us to be men and women of God, to fight the good fight, to stand fast in the faith, to be strong in the Lord in the midst of the battle, in the midst of this dark and evil world.

Those who ignore this call and the battle that rages around them are doomed to be casualties. We cannot remain neutral. We must choose sides. We must align ourselves with the forces of God, the forces of good. We must answer the bugle call, we must put on our armor and stand our ground—or the battle will roll over us and in our defenseless, bewildered state, the forces of evil will trample us into the dust of the battlefield.

So we must learn to recognize how the dark systems of the devil work. But more than that, we must learn the processes of overcoming the systems of the devil—not by flesh and blood, not by joining committees, not by political action, not by taking up clubs or assault weapons and attacking a human enemy. No, Paul says the weapons of our warfare are not flesh and blood weapons, not physical weapons, not political weapons. Rather, our weapons are mighty, through God, unto the pulling down of strongholds and bringing into captivity every thought to the obedience of Christ (2 Corinthians 10:3–5). That is the path to victory!

Do you think that is not challenging? That is the greatest challenge any ear could ever hear! Do you think that is not demanding? It demands more courage and sacrifice than any other cause in the history of the world! Do you think that is not exciting? It is the most exciting call that has ever gone out to men and women anywhere!

"Be strong in the Lord and in his mighty power!"

## Prayer

Gracious Father, thank You for a truth that startles me, prods me, and disturbs me. Thank You, Lord, for Your word of reality that speaks to me in the midst of my complacency and illusion. How easily I would drift on in futile ignorance, never raising a finger against the deterioration of life and the destruction of body and soul, were it not for this word of challenge that calls me back and makes me see life as it really is. Lord, teach me to bow in humility before Your Word and to say to the Holy Spirit, "O great Teacher of God, open these Scriptures and make them real to me today."

In Christ's name, amen.

*When a strong man, fully armed, guards his own house, his possessions are safe. But when someone stronger attacks and overpowers him, he takes away the armor in which the man trusted and divides up the spoils.*

*He who is not with me is against me, and he who does not gather with me, scatters.*

**Luke 11:21–23**

# 2

# Beginning the Battle

ROBERT THE BRUCE was king of Scotland from 1306 to 1329. Early in his reign, King Edward I of England invaded his nation, defeated his army, and forced him into hiding. While on the run, Robert the Bruce took refuge in a cave.

Completely disheartened, the Scottish king lay by a fire in the cave, ready to resign himself to complete defeat and the loss of his kingdom. But then, in the flickering firelight, he noticed a spider on the cave wall, spinning a web. The spider repeatedly attempted to secure the web, then failed, attempted again, then failed. Finally, the spider was able to anchor the web, making it strong and secure.

In the persistence of the spider, the Scottish king saw a metaphor of his own struggle against the English invader. He decided he would not allow himself to be defeated by past failures—he had to continue the fight for Scottish freedom. Robert the Bruce left his cave, led his troops across the field of battle, and defeated the English invaders at the Battle of Bannockburn in 1314. He continued to persevere for the next fourteen years until he finally won Scottish independence in 1328.

No battle was ever won without courage, perseverance, and strength. And that is the challenge before us, clearly sounded in Ephesians 6. Paul calls us to be strong in the Lord. He calls us to understand the nature of our enemy, those wicked spirits in high places who lie behind the insoluble problem of human evil. And he calls us to put on our armor and join the battle.

The apostle Paul indicates that the only ones who can successfully battle against the devil's forces are Christians. He writes, "For our struggle is not against flesh and blood . . ." The pronoun "our" in that statement refers not to "us," the human race in general, but to "us" Christians, followers of Jesus Christ. While the entire world is oppressed by the powers of evil, only Christians *struggle* against those powers. This is the consistent teaching throughout the Bible. The Bible indicates that all human beings are *victims* of these invisible forces, but only believers can be *victors* over them.

## No threat from within

Jesus Himself makes this point absolutely clear. There is a story in Luke of our Lord's reaction to the challenge that was presented to Him as He was casting out demons. His ministry of delivering people from demons was continually questioned by those who chose to approach the Scriptures intellectually. They did not like this business of casting out demons, and they tried to explain it in various ways. Some said His ability to cast out demons came from a relationship with Beelzebub, the prince of demons—

another name for Satan. They said it was by Satan's power that he was casting out demons.

The name Beelzebub means "lord of the garbage." The Jews regarded hell as a cosmic garbage dump, and in a real sense they were right, for that is exactly what hell is—a dumping ground for wasted lives. And because a garbage pile always attracts flies, they called Beelzebub "The Lord of the Flies." These people were accusing Jesus of casting out demons by the authority of Beelzebub, the Lord of the Flies.

But Jesus said, in effect, "No, you're quite wrong. In fact, what you are saying is not even logical. If that were true, then obviously Satan's kingdom would be divided against itself, and Satan would actually be pitted against the demons under his authority. That makes no sense at all!" Jesus states very simply that Satan never fights against himself. He is too clever, too cunning, and far too astute to divide his forces in that way. Satan knows that if he divided his own kingdom, his kingdom would fall.

Jesus is suggesting, therefore, that any one who was under the control of Satan has no hope of deliverance apart from an outside, intervening force. Here's how He puts it: "When a strong man, fully armed, guards his own house, his possessions are safe" (Luke 11:21). Who is the "strong man"? It is Satan. What is the "house"? The world. Who are the "goods"? The human race. In Luke 11:21–23, which presents this figure of the strong man, three great principles emerge:

(1) *Humanity, alone against Satan, is powerless and hopeless.* That is the unchanging position of Scripture. John says, "We [Christians] know that we are children of God,

and that the whole world is under the control of the evil one" (1 John 5:19).

The Bible tells us that the world has fallen under the control of Satan. What does the Bible mean by "the world"? Not the world of trees and mountains and lakes and seas— that is God's world. No, the Bible speaks of the world of organized human society, which has fallen under the control of Satan. We, as worldlings, are trapped within this domain of the evil one, and there is no possibility of escape apart from an intervention from without. For, as Jesus says, "When a strong man, fully armed, guards his own house, his possessions are safe." There can be no threat from within to Satan's control.

It is here that our Lord puts His finger on the reason for the continual failure of the usual methods men and women employ to correct evils and wrongs. Human methods of reform fail because they do not come to grips with the essential problem. All our efforts to correct the evils we see in life are simply rearrangements of the difficulties. We succeed only in stirring them around a bit until they take a different form. Our methods can never solve the essential problem of evil because they cannot come to grips with the power of Satan. We cannot threaten Satan from within his dominion; only a stronger, outside agency can threaten the stranglehold of the evil one on our world and our lives.

As C. S. Lewis so aptly put it, "No clever arrangement of bad eggs will make a good omelet." And when the full cycle of problems is run through, it begins again, and we say, "History repeats itself."

What are the usual methods of human reform? You can list them easily. Almost invariably they are *legislation, education,* and an *improved environment.* Every problem we face is usually approached by using one of these reforms, if not all three combined. Legislation is law—the attempt to control the behavior of the outward man. Law alone can do nothing to alter the inward man. It does not change the basic nature of man but merely restricts him under certain conditions.

Education is one of the worst so-called remedies for a deranged personality or a twisted mind. Scripture tells us that we are all are born into this world with twisted minds. (Some are more twisted than others, which is why most of us consider ourselves "normal," while thinking the other fellow is the one who is "twisted"!) To educate a twisted mind is but to make it more clever in its wickedness. The educated criminal is a far more clever, far more subtle, and far more dangerous than the ignorant criminal. The educated mind may have a thin veneer of erudition or sophistication hiding his corrupt personality from view, but the corruption is there nonetheless. Education does not change the core of a man or woman—it only makes him or her more clever, and potentially more destructive.

An improved environment does not change a person either. When you take a man out of the slums, for example, and put him into a nicer environment, you do absolutely nothing to the man himself. In a little while he'll make that new environment the slum as well. So taking a man out of the slums does not necessarily take the slums out of the man.

This is not to say that these reforms have no value. We should have laws for the sake of an orderly society. We should have education for the sake of a literate and effective society. And we should improve the living conditions of all men and women, for the sake of a just, compassionate, and decent society. But let's not make the mistake of thinking that these reforms will lead us to Utopia, to a shining new society of love and brotherhood. None of these reforms can produce a Utopia, because none of them has the power to transform human nature and the inner human being. None of them can counteract the invisible spiritual forces that are at war against us.

That is why so many of our best and brightest thinkers have arrived at a point of despair after a lifetime of trying to change humanity through legislative, educational, and social reform. They invariably end up in a pit of pessimism and despair. Listen to these words of Bertrand Russell, the high priest of the cult of social reformers and free thinkers:

> The life of man is a long march through the night, surrounded by invisible foes, tortured by weariness and pain, toward a goal that you can hope to reach and where none can tarry long. One by one as they march our comrades vanish from our side, seized by the silent orders of omnipotent death. Brief and powerless is man's life. On him and all his race the slow, sure doom falls, pitiless and dark. Blind to good and evil, reckless of destruction, omnipotent matter roles on its relentless way. For man, condemned today to lose his dearest, tomorrow himself to pass through the gates of darkness, it remains only to cherish, ere yet the blow falls, the lofty thoughts that ennoble his little day.

Those eloquent but bleak words catalog the sheer despair into which humanity falls apart from God. There is a growing sense of despair everywhere you turn today. That despair is the unconscious realization of man's helplessness under Satan.

Now look at our Lord's words in Luke 11:22: "But when someone stronger attacks and overpowers him, he takes away the armor in which the man trusted and divides up the spoils." Who is this "someone stronger"? It is Jesus. He is speaking of Himself. He says that when a strong man, fully armed, guards his palace, his goods are at peace and nothing can be done about it, least of all by the goods themselves. But when One who is stronger comes, He breaks the power of Satan.

Here's the next principle the Lord reveals in this passage:

(2) *Only the "good news" of the gospel of Jesus Christ can break the grip of the "bad news" of the devil.* We sing of this truth in that great hymn of the faith, "O For a Thousand Tongues":

> He breaks the power of canceled sin,
> He sets the prisoner free;
> His blood can make the foulest clean,
> His blood availed for me.

We have been born into a world under the control of the satanic mind. Yet, in the mystery of the cross of Jesus and in the power of His resurrection, applied by faith, we discover that the force which ruins us is now broken and its power is canceled.

That is why this Christian gospel is so exclusive. That is why Christians are perfectly justified by the Word of God when they say there is no other answer to the problems of man; that there is no other power that can touch the basic problem of human life. Many people say that there are many roads to God, that it doesn't matter what you believe or who you believe in, as long as you are "sincere." But Jesus is very clear on this point: There's only one "stronger one" who has come into the world and is capable of breaking the power of this dark spirit, setting us free from the evil one's dominion and domination. No one can come to God the Father, and to freedom from the dominion of the evil one, except through Jesus alone (John 14:6). He is the "stronger one." There is no other.

Actress Grace Lee Whitney can testify to the fact that the "stronger one," Jesus Christ, has come into her life to set her free from the evil power that rules this world. In the 1950s and 1960s, she appeared in numerous motion pictures and television shows, working with the biggest stars in Hollywood—Marilyn Monroe, Groucho Marx, Jack Lemmon, Robert Stack, and many more.

Then, in 1966, she was tapped to play a featured part on TV's *Star Trek*. During the first season, however, after appearing in only thirteen episodes, her character, Yeoman Janice Rand, was written out of the show. The sense of failure and rejection she felt after losing the role sent her into a tailspin of alcoholism, drug abuse, and immorality. She got to the point where she was drinking on skid row street corners right out of the bottle. Hospitalized, she was told by her doctors that the gin she had been drinking was eating a hole in her esophagus, and had nearly destroyed her liver. If she didn't stop drinking, they said, she would be dead within a couple weeks. Grace Lee Whitney was scared—but she didn't know how to stop drinking. The alcohol controlled her.

A friend took her to a recovery group, where she was introduced to God. The group said the Lord's Prayer together, and at that very moment this prayer that had always sounded like gibberish to her suddenly made perfect sense. It was the first time she ever really knew that God cared for her—and she immediate stopped drinking and using drugs. In the weeks that followed, God led her on a journey to Israel. On a walking tour outside of Jerusalem, she came to a gate with a sign that read "Garden of Gethsemane." In her autobiography, *The Longest Trek*, Grace Lee Whitney recalls what happened next,

> I put my hands on the iron bars of the gate and looked through, into the Garden of Gethsemane. Suddenly, I felt weak, as if I was about to faint. I had to hold onto the bars to remain standing.
>
> Then I saw Jesus.
>
> He was beyond the iron bars, praying in the garden....
>
> I thought, *But I'm Jewish!*
>
> As if He could read my mind, He turned and looked at me. "So am I," He said.

After that experience, Grace Lee Whitney gave her heart and life to the Lord Jesus Christ. The "stronger man" came into her life with amazing power, setting her free from her addictions, her enslavement to immorality, her guilt and shame. Today, she goes to *Star Trek* conventions and women's prisons and television talk shows, telling everyone who will listen about the Lord and what He has done in her life.

And Grace Lee Whitney is just one among thousands who can testify to the power of Jesus Christ, the "stronger man." Only He has the power to invade the devil's domain and liberate people—the devil's "possessions"—so that they can become the cherished, prized possessions of God! Those who have such testimonies include not only alcoholics and drug addicts and people who have lived in outrageous immorality, but also people whose habits are less spectacular but no less sinful, including "church people" with evil habits and attitudes of anger, lust, self-righteousness, and pride.

The strongest chains are not those that can be placed around the body, but those that are wrapped around the mind and heart. The writers of Scripture make this clear. Paul tells us, "The god of this age has blinded the minds of the unbelievers" (2 Corinthians 4:4). And that great document on human liberty, Paul's letter to the Romans, opens with the same basic thought—that human beings in their darkened state, under the dominion of the evil one, have engaged in all manner of evil practices, leaving God no choice but to give them what they demand: "He gave them over to a depraved mind, to do what ought not to be done" (Romans 1:28). Paul suggests that the great hatred we see exhibited against God and His gospel does not come from the uneducated but from the educated: "Although they claimed to be wise, they became fools" (Romans 1:22), and so they "exchanged the truth of God for a lie" (Romans 1:25).

Into this realm of spiritual darkness and self-willed resistance to the will and goodness of God, Jesus Christ has come to set us free. John says that Jesus came into the world "to destroy the devil's work" (1 John 3:8). There is no adequate explanation of His coming apart from that. Paul says that Jesus has "rescued us from the dominion of darkness and brought us into the kingdom of the Son he loves" (Colossians 1:13).

Paul himself was chosen as an apostle to the Gentiles, and in a dramatic conversion experience on the road to Damascus, he said to the Lord whom he saw in His glory, "Who are you, Lord?" And after identifying himself, Jesus replied, "Stand on your feet. I have appeared to you to appoint you as a servant and as a witness of what you have seen of me and what I will show you. . . . I am sending you to [your own people] to open their eyes and turn them from darkness to light, and from the power of Satan to God" (Acts 26:15–18).

This is the principal purpose of the gospel. If we try to channel it first into the smaller areas of life, such as applying it to social concerns, we only reveal how far we have mistaken its purpose. The gospel will ultimately find its way into the social condition of humanity, because the gospel of Jesus Christ is pervasive. Once it gets a hold of us, it doesn't let go until we are transformed through and through.

But the gospel must first make its impact on this basic problem of human life. Humanity is in the grip of an evil power, and we are helpless to free ourselves from bondage to that power by our own strength. The only one who can deliver us from it is Jesus Christ. He has already done so in the mystery of His cross and through the power and glory of His resurrection.

When a person trusts in Christ and commits himself to Christ, he discovers that the gospel becomes real and practical in his own experience. This is what we call "conversion." But conversion is only the beginning of the battle. Very soon, a new Christian becomes aware of the evil forces at work to destroy him. If he goes no farther in his new life than to believe his sins are forgiven, he will remain in bondage to those sins, living a life of conflict and frustration. But the battle is fought on the ground that we have been delivered from the dominion of darkness—that we have been brought out of the power of Satan and into the kingdom of God.

Returning to the passage in Luke, we have seen (1) that human beings alone are helpless against the power of Satan, and (2) that liberation from the power of Satan is available only through the gospel, through belief in Jesus Christ, who destroyed Satan's power. Now we come to the Lord's third principle, revealed in Luke 11:23: "He who is not with me is against me, and he who does not gather with me, scatters" (Luke 11:23). Here, then, is the next principle Jesus reveals to us:

(3) *There is no neutrality in spiritual warfare. You either stand with Christ—or against Him.* He is saying here that it is not possible to take a neutral stance. Mere profession is not sufficient; total commitment is required. There are always those who say, "I understand something of the gospel, and I agree that there's much of value in the Christian faith. I am a friend of Christianity. I believe that Christianity exerts a positive influence on society—but I do not care to go so far as to personally 'receive Christ.' I don't want to be thought 'extreme' or a 'religious fanatic.' I choose to remain neutral."

Jesus says this stance is impossible. There is no neutrality. "He who is not with me is against me." A person who does not receive total deliverance is still under the bondage and control of the dark powers of Satan. There are no exceptions.

That is why Christ is the crisis of history. He spoke of Himself that way—as the divider of humanity. As He looks at human beings, there are only two groups. There are those who are wholly with Him because they are of Him— they have received Him, they know Him, they love Him, and they partake in His life. And there are those who are against Him. "He who is not *with* me is *against* me."

On the other hand, some are tempted to say, "Well, if this is the case, then I want to be a Christian, but I don't know about all this inward control. I'm willing to go along with the outward forms of Christianity—I'm willing to join the church—but inwardly, I still believe in directing my own life and running my own affairs." Jesus says you cannot do that. "He who does not gather with me, scatters."

Let me tell you a tragic story. Lord Kenneth Clark (1903–1983) was a world-renowned art historian and host of the BBC-PBS television series *Civilisation*. He lived his life as an agnostic. As far as we can know, he died without faith in Jesus Christ. In his autobiography, he told about the experience of visiting a magnificent European cathedral, where he had what he described as a profound and breathtaking religious experience. "My whole being," he recalled, "was irradiated by a kind of heavenly joy far more intense than anything I had known before."

Yet, immediately after this experience, Clark pulled back from faith in Christ. He realized that if he were to become a Christian, his entire life would have to change. He liked the life he had as an agnostic, and did not want to submit his life to the lordship of Jesus Christ. Besides, he said, his family and friends were all as irreligious as he was, and they would think he had lost his mind. He didn't want to subject himself to their ridicule, so he rejected God and turned his back on his one brief glimmering of Christian joy. "I was too deeply embedded in the world to change course," he reflected.

What a tragic epitaph for a human soul! And how many people around us could say those same words: "I refuse to change—I am too deeply embedded in the world." Here was a man with a great reputation in the world—yet he chose to waste his mortal life and his eternal soul pursuing things that could never last and never satisfy. What if, instead of choosing to be accepted by his godless family members and friends, he had chosen to have an influence upon them for Christ? What if instead of choosing to squander and scatter God's gift of life, he had chosen instead to gather his family and friends into the kingdom of God?

There is one thing that reveals whether you're with Jesus or against Him: the influence of your life. Jesus Christ has come into the world to gather together the adopted children of God. His is a gathering influence, breaking down divisions, binding hearts together, reuniting families, making people live together in harmony, breaking down the barriers of race, healing wounds, bringing nations together, drawing men, women, and children to Himself.

### Victor or victim?

The great question of your life and mine is: "What is the essential character of your life? Is it self-centeredness—or self-givingness? Are you with Christ or against him? Are you gathering with him in a healing, wholesome ministry—or are you a divisive force in your family, your church, or your neighborhood? Do you split people up or bring people together?

You say you're a Christian. All right. Are your children drawn closer to faith in Christ because of your example? Or are they turned away by the example you set? Do your children and your spouse see Christ living in you—or do they see only *you*, your demands, your ill-temper, your pettiness, and your selfishness? These are crucial questions that each of us must answer.

Our Lord cuts right to the core of life. Our lives are laid absolutely bare before Him and we are ultimately judged on the basis of our relationship to Him. The evidence of that relationship is the influence we exercise in our families, our church, our neighborhood, our workplace, and wherever we are involved in the lives of other people.

The question you and I must ask ourselves is, "Am I a victor, or a victim?" In our own strength, we are helpless to escape the dominion of the evil one. We are not free. We are not able to carry out our own decisions, except in a limited area, and this illusion of freedom makes us imagine that we are free, unrestrained individuals. The Bible tells us that apart from Christ we are under the unbroken influence of an evil force that influences our thoughts and reactions. The only way of escape is through the One who has come to destroy the works of the devil.

If you have not known that deliverance, you can do it now. Perhaps as you have been reading, you have had to say, "If all this is true, then I am still an unbeliever. I am still under the power of Satan." In that case, the message of the gospel to you is this: In one moment of time you can pass from death into life. In one moment of commitment, trusting only Christ and His work, not in your own efforts to be "good enough," you can say, "Lord, here am I. Save me." The moment you pray that prayer, you pass from death into life. That is what conversion is. In those words you will open the door that allows the Lord Jesus to accomplish His saving work in your life.

### Prayer

Father, may those who have been seeking answers pass now from the power of Satan into the kingdom of God. May they be delivered and set free. For me, Lord, who has already experienced this and who knows the reality of this delivering power in my life, I pray that I may never forget that I have been set free. I ask that you continually remind me that Jesus did for me what I could never do for myself. May I have a heart filled with love for Him who loved me and gave Himself for me.

In the name of Jesus, who set me free, amen.

*As for you, you were dead in your transgressions and sins, in which you used to live when you followed the ways of this world and of the ruler of the kingdom of the air, the spirit who is now at work in those who are disobedient.*

**Ephesians 2:1–2**

*Put on the full armor of God so that you can take your stand against the devil's schemes.*

**Ephesians 6:11**

# 3

# The Strategy of Satan

ONE OF THE MOST STUNNING VICTORIES in the annals of warfare occurred in 1991, with the defeat of Iraqi strongman Saddam Hussein and the liberation of Kuwait during the Gulf War. Military historians tell us that one of the most important reasons that war was won so decisively (Allied losses: 149 versus Iraqi losses of 100,000 or more) and quickly (only 100 hours) was that the allied forces had a clear, in-depth understanding of Saddam Hussein's military strategy and were able to thwart the Iraqi dictator at every turn.

When the military commanders of the allied coalition learned that Saddam planned simply to replay the same strategy he used in the 1980–88 war with Iran, they knew exactly how to defeat him. The Allied generals, led by General Norman Schwarzkopf, devised a strategy of encirclement. Even though Saddam's army outnumbered the coalition forces two to one and were well dug into their desert fortifications, the allied coalition used a combination

49

of superior placement, superior firepower and technology, speed, and misdirection to defeat Iraq.

While U.S. Marines conspicuously practiced for a seaborne invasion along the Kuwaiti coast, drawing Saddam's attention in the wrong direction, the main coalition force was massed for an invasion across the desert. Knowing the exact location of Saddam's tanks and artillery, the coalition pounded those locations with everything from bombers to helicopters. Knowing that Saddam's forces were dug in behind sand berms and other entrenchments, allied troops practiced bulldozing and storming similar desert barricades until they could do it in their sleep.

Once the war began, Iraqi troops began surrendering so eagerly that the Allies didn't know where to put them all. In one case, a pair of Iraqi armored vehicles encountered a lone U.S. soldier whose vehicle was stuck in the sand. The soldier expected to be shot or captured—but instead, the Iraqis surrendered to him and helped him get his vehicle unstuck!

The story of the 100-hour war in the Persian Gulf is an apt metaphor to describe our spiritual warfare against Satan. Though the devil would have us believe he is invincible, his cause has already been doomed by the cross of Christ. If we understand his strategy, the victory will be ours. In the end, we will have the honor of standing with our Commander-in-Chief, the Lord Jesus, and hear him declare that this raging tyrant, the devil, was no match for the forces of heaven.

In spiritual warfare as in human warfare, the key to victory is to *know your enemy*—and *know his strategies*.

## Armed with cruel hate

As we have seen in the preceding chapter, the Bible clearly shows that all human beings, without exception, are helpless victims of satanic control, apart from Jesus Christ. Under the domination of invisible satanic forces, human beings are oppressed and unhappy and incapable of escape by any wisdom or power of their own. But the good news is that we can be set free by the outside intervention of Jesus Himself, who came "to destroy the works of the devil." He has broken the power and bondage of Satan over human lives. When we receive Him into our lives, we are liberated to live as children of God.

It is important to understand what this liberation truly means. It does not mean that we have been set free to live lives of selfishness and self-indulgence. That is a common misconception, but it is nowhere taught in the Bible.

No, we haven't been liberated to live for ourselves. We have been liberated to live for our Commander, Jesus Christ. We have been set free so that we can join the battle! That is the call which comes to all Christians. And understand: When God calls us to join the battle, He is not using a mere metaphor. This war is real, the enemy is determined to destroy us, and his weapons are deadly. Like soldiers in any war, we stand a chance suffering wounds at the hands of our enemy. To better defend ourselves against this implacable foe, we need to understand the way he operates.

The first step for any soldier in training is to learn about the strategy and weapons the enemy will use against him. The devil is a cunning and wily strategist, and that is why Martin Luther wrote these stirring words:

For still our ancient foe
   Doth seek to work us woe—
His craft and power are great,
   And, armed with cruel hate,
On earth is not his equal.


The record of Scripture confirms this truth. Read the Old Testament and you'll see that every saint, every prophet, every patriarch, every one of the great and glorious kings of Israel, was defeated at one time or another by the devil. The wisest and greatest of men are absolutely helpless in attempting to out-wit the devil by themselves. Yet, as we have already seen, the Bible makes it clear that we can walk in victory. God does not want us to fail; that is why He has made victory possible in our lives.

James says, "Resist the devil, and he will flee from you" (James 4:7). Think of that! This clever, cunning strategist who has held the world in defeat for centuries, whom no man is able to out-maneuver, will *flee* from you when you learn not to be ignorant of his schemes and strategies.

Now, the question we must ask ourselves is, "What is the strategy of the devil? How does he plan to defeat us? How does he keep the world in such bondage? And what are the particular ways he uses to neutralize my effectiveness for God?" The only one in all history who has ever consistently defeated the devil, not only in His life but also in His death, is the Lord Jesus Christ. He put His finger squarely upon the strategy and tactics of Satan when He said that the devil "was a murderer from the beginning, not holding to the truth, for there is no truth in him. When he lies, he speaks his native language, for he is a liar and the father of lies" (John 8:44). The strategy of the devil is to murder. The tactic by which he accomplishes this is to lie.

How does the devil plan to oppose the work of God in the world? By murdering, by destroying. One of the names given to the devil in the book of the Revelation is *Apollyon*, which means "Destroyer." What is it to destroy? It is to create chaos, to lay waste, to ruin, to make desolate. There you have the explanation for the whole tragic story of human history: A Destroyer is at work among human beings.

Our God is a God of beauty, harmony, order, perfection, love, light, and grace. There is enough evidence left in the world of nature, including our own being, and in the world of ideas, to see this marvelous symmetry, beauty, and perfection of God. The Lord is a God of harmony and order. The world was created as orderly and perfect—and even human beings were once orderly and perfect.

But then a Destroyer came on the scene. It is his delight to smash, mangle, twist, mutilate, disfigure, darken, and blast in every way he can. It does not make any difference whether it is bodies or souls, flesh or ideas, matter or spirit—the aim of the devil is exactly the same in every case. That is why the devil can never offer anything positive to human life. He can create nothing. He has never made anything, and he never will make anything. All he can do is destroy what God has made. His power is totally negative and destructive in every way.

What are the tactics the devil employs? He destroys by deceiving, by lying, by distorting, by counterfeiting, by masquerading, by clouding human minds with illusion and fantasy. This is what Paul calls "the devil's schemes," or as some translations put it, "the wiles of the devil." Read through the Bible and see how many times the work of the devil is referred to in that manner—the snares and the traps of the devil, the lies and illusions, the stratagems and the wiles. That is why we must look closely at the tactics the devil uses against us—so that we can be strong and well-defended when he comes to us to defeat us, weaken us, and ruin our lives.

## Direct and indirect attacks

The Bible makes it clear that the tactics of the devil fall into two major divisions: direct attack and indirect attack. He is capable of direct confrontation with human beings, as well as a subtle, indirect approach. The devil uses these two methods to maintain worldwide control over the race of humanity. The Bible indicates that there are fallen hosts of angels called "demons," whom Paul refers to when he writes, "For our struggle is not against flesh and blood, but against the rulers, against the authorities, against the powers of this dark world and against the spiritual forces of evil in the heavenly realms" (Ephesians 6:12).

It is crucial to understand that the phrase "heavenly realms" does not refer to heaven, God's eternal place of glory, the final home of every believer. In this context, "heavenly" refers to the spiritual realm, or more literally "the realm of the invisibilities," the invisible realities of life. The devil and his hosts are not visible, but they are very real. The devil's activity is in this realm of the invisible reality of life, the heavenly places, where God works.

The Bible tells us very little of the origin of the devil and his angels. But there is enough written to suggest that the devil was a being created originally as an angel of might, strength, beauty, and power. There is a brief reference to the fall of this great angel, whose name was Lucifer, and who became lifted up by pride. Pride is always the mark of the devil. Seized by pride, he chose to rival God and, in doing so, he fell from his station of honor and beauty—and he became the devil. The Old Testament prophet relates the fall of Satan with these words:

> How you have fallen from heaven,
>> O morning star [Lucifer], son of the dawn!
> You have been cast down to the earth,
>> you who once laid low the nations!
> You said in your heart,
>> "I will ascend to heaven;
> I will raise my throne above the stars of God;
> I will sit enthroned on the mount of assembly,
>> on the utmost heights of the sacred mountain.
> I will ascend above the tops of the clouds;
>> I will make myself like the Most High."
> But you are brought down to the grave,
>> to the depths of the pit (Isaiah 14:12–15).

And in the New Testament, there is a scene in which Jesus sends out seventy-two disciples to exercise His authority and further His ministry. They return with a triumphant report: "Lord, even the demons submit to us in your name" (Luke 10:17). And Jesus replies that this is to be expected, because of who He Himself is—the eternal One who was there at creation, and who has witnessed all of history, including Satan's fall. "I saw Satan fall like lightning from heaven," Jesus told them (Luke 10:18).

In his fall, Satan drew a third of the angels with him, and those fallen angels constitute the principalities and powers, the organized kingdom of darkness, as opposed to the kingdom of God. It is through these hosts of wicked spirits that Satan is able to make a direct assault upon human life.

This direct assault covers what the Bible refers to as "demon possession," the outright control of a human personality by the power of a wicked spirit. It also extends to such activities as soothsaying, occultism, spiritism (or spiritualism), and is related black magic arts such as astrology, horoscopes, voodooism, fortune-telling, witchcraft (wicca), shamanism, paganism, channeling, and the like.

A strong word of warning is in order here. There is no question that there is a great deal of fraud and deception in this whole field of black magic, channeling, and fortune-telling. There are charlatans at work who make their living off the superstitious fears of people, and they use deceptive tricks to fool people into thinking they are genuinely in touch with spirits and occult powers. It is very difficult to tell the difference between the genuine and the false in this field. Great skepticism, care, and clear thinking must be used by anyone attempting to investigate this dark realm. While there is a great deal of smoke and mirrors in the occult domain, the Bible tells us there is considerable fire as well. Despite the existence of fraud, there is truth—dangerous truth—behind the operation of black magic and witchcraft.

The Bible consistently warns us against dabbling in these matters. Here are just a few examples of biblical teaching on the subject:

"Do not turn to mediums or seek out spiritists, for you will be defiled by them. I am the LORD your God" (Leviticus 19:31).

"I will set my face against the person who turns to mediums and spiritists to prostitute himself by following them, and I will cut him off from his people" (Leviticus 20:6).

When men tell you to consult mediums and spiritists, who whisper and mutter, should not a people inquire of their God? Why consult the dead on behalf of the living? (Isaiah 8:19).

Under the Old Testament law, the people of Israel were strictly forbidden from having anything to do with wizards who speak in spells and incantations, who try to make contact with the dead, or who deal with the world of the occult. This prohibition was largely because any investigation into this realm immediately lays one open to powers beyond human understanding and makes it possible for demonic power to subdue the will of that person. This is dangerous ground. In fact, it often progressively opens the way to outright demon possession.

## The devil's direct attack: demon possession

Many people are incredulous and disbelieving that there is such a thing as demon possession. "Surely you don't believe in such nonsense anymore," they say. "In this educated, sophisticated day and age, you don't really mean to suggest that there are such things as demons! After all, the Bible was written in ancient times for gullible, primitive people. We are much better informed today. What was once called demon possession we now know to be mental illness, and we can treat it with drugs and other therapies." The biblical reply to that kind of thinking can be expressed in three principles:

(1) *The Bible is not a book of primitive superstition; on the contrary, the Bible carefully differentiates between mental illness and demon possession.* The writers of the Scriptures were certainly aware of this distinction. One of them, Luke (who was a physician), was certainly acquainted with the distinctions between physical diseases and mental illnesses and demon possession (see Luke 4:40–41). In Matthew also, a careful distinction is made between those who were afflicted by diseases, those who were demon-possessed, and those who were mentally ill (see Matthew 4:24).

(2) *Biblical cases of demon possession do not conform to the clinical pattern of any known mental disease.* There are diseases of the body, there are diseases of the mind—and then, quite distinctly, there is demon possession. Diseases of the mind, like those of the body, present standard clinical patterns and symptoms that can be readily recognized. But when you carefully examine the biblical accounts of demon possession, you find that these accounts do not fit any of the standard patterns of mental diseases. Mental illness and demon possession are clearly not the same thing.

In contrast to mental illness, biblical cases of demon possession always contain an element of debasement. There is uncleanness and moral defilement present.

Also in the biblical accounts of demon possession we see an immediate recognition by the demon of the character and identity of the Lord Jesus Christ. When Christ would deliver people from demons, those demons would often call out and say (as, for example, in Luke 4:34)— "What do you want with us, Jesus of Nazareth? Have you come to destroy us? I know who you are—the Holy One of God!" The demons used titles for Jesus which the human victims of possession could not know. Though demons are in opposition to God, they inhabit the invisible realm and are well acquainted with spiritual realities; only such creatures could have instantly recognized the authority of Jesus Christ.

Further, there is always the presence of a totally distinct and different personality involved. In some cases multiple demonic personalities are involved, as in the incident where Jesus asks the name of the demon and the demon's reply is, "My name is Legion, for we are many" (Mark 5:9).

Finally, we see that Jesus is able to transfer demons from individuals to animals—something that is never observed in cases of mental illness. How do you explain the case of the Gadarene swine? If demon possession is merely mental sickness or a hallucination or some kind of schizophrenia, then how did the demons leave the man, enter the herd of swine, and send them rushing to drown themselves in the sea? These cases simply do not conform to any clinical pattern of known mental disease.

(3) *Jesus Himself described these cases as demon possession, and he treated them that way.* In sending out His disciples, He gave them authority to cast out demons. "Well," some would argue, "we have an explanation for that. Jesus was simply accommodating Himself to the way of thinking of the people of His day. They believed in demons and devils,

so He simply spoke in those same terms." But it is impossible to take that position and be consistent with the rest the account of Christ's ministry, for we see Him constantly correcting misconceptions like that. On one occasion He said to His disciples concerning another matter, "If it were not so, I would have told you" (John 14:2). He did not come to coddle the superstitions and misconceptions of His hearers; rather, He came to reveal the truth about the world as it really is.

Throughout the Christian centuries there have been various outbreaks of demon possession described by missionaries in many lands. It is a rather commonplace phenomenon in many places in our world today. And it is significant, I think, that whenever Christian teaching spreads, the direct assault of these evil powers upon human life is kept in check. Even secular teaching, when it is moral and uplifting and based upon the Bible and Christian values, demonstrates an ability to keep these manifestations under control.

But when education becomes purely secular and denies the Bible and God, then—even though men and women reject superstition and profess a degree of sophistication about these matters—all this is not enough to keep these powers at bay. As our world grows more and more godless and secularized, we will witness an increasing tide of demonic manifestation in our culture—guaranteed. There is no power in man to withhold these forces or to stand against them, because this is the manifestation of the god of this world.

When we, as Christians, are confronted with what we suspect is demon possession, the one thing we're told to do to help such people is to pray. These cases of demon possession, Jesus said, yield to concerted and persistent prayer. There is no need to chant or sprinkle holy water or conduct exorcism rituals, as the sensationalized Hollywood horror movies portray. Prayer is the recommended therapy in any case of this type. Let us give ourselves to prayer and nothing else.

For the sake of a balanced perspective, I hasten to say that there seems to be too much concern among Christians about the matter of demon possession. I know certain Christians who feel they must "bind Satan" before they do anything. When they go into a room to have a meeting, they pray to bind the powers of darkness. I know others who ascribe every common problem of human life to some manifestation of demon activity. The New Testament offers no justification for this type of approach.

The New Testament letters of the apostles seldom mention the direct attack of Satan against human beings. There are a few instances of this sort of attack, but after our Lord physically left the world there seems to be a reduction in the evidence of demonic activity. As we see in the four Gospels, these dark powers were no doubt stirred up by His presence on earth, but they seem to be less active as we move through the book of Acts and on into the letters of Paul and the other apostles. There is much written about Satan's *indirect* attack in the letters of Paul, but Paul has little to say about the *direct* attack of satanic forces. Nowhere do we read that Christians should "bind" the powers of darkness before entering a room, nor that we should ascribe all the common problems of life to demonic activities. That idea is not in the New Testament.

By far, the majority of attacks of the devil against Christians are not direct but indirect. That is why they are called the "schemes" of the devil. Schemes suggest deviousness—acting in a way that is subtle, secretive, and treacherous. We need to examine this more thoroughly, for the major attack of the devil and his powers against human life is not by direct means, but indirectly—by satanic suggestions through the natural and commonplace situations of life.

## The devil's indirect attack: satanic subversion

The Bible tells us that the indirect approach of the devil comes largely through two means: "the world" and "the flesh." We often hear it said that the enemies of the Christian are the world, the flesh, and the devil, as though these were three equally powerful enemies. But there are not three. There is only one enemy, the devil, as Paul tells us in Ephesians 6. And our enemy, the devil, uses these two means, the world and the flesh, to make his indirect attack against us. Earlier in Ephesians, Paul addressed these words to Christians, including you and me:

> As for you, you were dead in your transgressions and sins, in which you used to live when you followed the ways of this world [the first channel] and of the ruler of the kingdom of the air [a description of the devil], the spirit who is now at work in those who are disobedient (Ephesians 2:1–2).

In other words, Paul is telling us, "Do not forget, you Christians, that you too once followed the course of this world—you were under the grip and in the control of the ruler of the power of the air, the evil spirit who continues to be at work in the nonChristians all around you." Paul goes on in to tell us in the next verse:

> All of us also lived among them at one time, gratifying the cravings of our sinful nature [or "the flesh" in the King James Version—the devil's second channel] and following its desires and thoughts. Like the rest, we were by nature objects of wrath (Ephesians 2:3).

The most basic of these two channels is "the flesh"— our sinful nature. When the Bible uses the term "the flesh," it does so in a symbolic sense. Many of us, when we approach middle-age, are troubled with too much flesh. But that is not the sense in which the Bible uses the term. "The flesh," in this context, is not our bodies, not the meat and blood and bones of our physical life. It is a term that describes the urge to self-centeredness within us, that distortion of human nature which makes us want to be our own god—the proud ego, the uncrucified self that is the seat of willful defiance and rebellion against authority.

We are all born with this sinful nature. None of us had to go to school to learn how to sin and be self-centered. Who taught us to lie? Who taught us to be proud and bitter and rebellious and defiant and self-centered? We never had to take classes in these. We're all experts in how to sin by the time we are ready to go to school. We are all born with "the flesh," and it is the presence of this sinful nature that makes us sinners.

James calls this the wisdom which is from beneath, which is "earthly, unspiritual, *of the devil*" (James 3:15). It is the devil—attacking indirectly through the essentially sinful character of our human nature. Paul says in Romans, as J. B. Phillips translates it, "everyone has sinned; everyone falls short of the beauty of God's plan" (Romans 3:23).

"The world," on the other hand, is the corporate expression of all the flesh-centered individuals who make up the human race. Since the flesh is in every human being—acting in a way that is satanic, sensual, and earthly—the total combined expression of such beings constitutes the world and determines the philosophy of the world. It is that tremendous pressure of the majority upon the minority to conform, adjust, keep in step, and go along with the crowd.

When the Bible addresses itself to Christians, it says, "Do not conform any longer to the pattern of this world" (Romans 12:2). In other words, "Do not let the world squeeze you into its mold." Why? Because the world is flesh-centered, flesh-governed, and as Jesus said to Nicodemus, "Flesh gives birth to flesh, but the Spirit gives birth to spirit" (John 3:6). In order to be changed, people must be born of the Spirit. So this is the world—that human society which insists on satanic value judgments and is guided by satanic pride and philosophy. While the world is totally unaware of it, nevertheless, it is under the control of satanic philosophy.

We must never forget the ultimate goal of these clever strategies: the devil seeks to destroy, ruin, and make waste. That is his purpose toward you and me. You can probably think of people—people who were once full of promising potential—who have given the devil some toe-hold in their lives, and the devil has used it to destroy their lives. Perhaps they got involved in some habit that took over their lives, such as drugs or promiscuous sex or pornography. Or perhaps they have ruined their families by their habitual rage or destructive tongue. Or perhaps they have turned aside from the truth of God in order to chase some worldly philosophy or wealth or prestige or self-centered idea of "fulfillment." It is a story that is repeated again and again, in life after tragic life: Satan schemes to destroy a life God loves—and in that particular life, Satan wins because that individual was not aware of the schemes of the devil.

So we have been called to a battle against a vicious, scheming, unseen enemy. We are called to battle not only for our own sakes, not only for our own families, but for the sake of others around us. We must warn those around us that life is a battle, and that the enemy has us in his crosshairs. We must warn one another to be aware of the devil's schemes, so that we can be armed and defended against the devil's attacks. And we must pray for one another, because our only true defender is Jesus Himself.

Battling against these forces of darkness is what makes human life possible on the earth. If Christians, who are the salt of the earth, were not devoted to an intense, intelligent battle against Satan and satanic forces, if we as believers did not choose to be strong in the Lord and in the power of his might, then human life could not exist on this planet. The forces of evil would run rampant and unopposed throughout human society, and life on earth would be a horrible, unendurable hell. It is the presence of Christians, and the Holy Spirit who lives within us, and the gospel that we bring, that makes the world as livable and bearable as it is, even for nonChristians.

So we have an enormous responsibility before God and before the entire world to give ourselves, body and soul, to this great battle against the schemes of the evil one. We have a responsibility to battle the schemes of the devil in this world, and to point the way to the peace and security that lies ahead of us in the world to come.

## Prayer

Thank You, Father, that the victory is already won. Thank You for revealing to me the strategy of my enemy—and for the assurance that I have already been brought out of darkness and into the kingdom of Your light. I no longer fight alone in a losing battle in my own fading strength. Instead, filled with Your strength and courage, I fight knowing that the battle has already been won upon the cross of Christ. Thank You for that victory!

In the name of Jesus Christ, my Victorious Commander, amen.

*Finally, be strong in the Lord and in his mighty power. Put on the full armor of God so that you can take your stand against the devil's schemes. For our struggle is not against flesh and blood, but against the rulers, against the authorities, against the powers of this dark world and against the spiritual forces of evil in the heavenly realms. Therefore put on the full armor of God, so that when the day of evil comes, you may be able to stand your ground, and after you have done everything, to stand.*

**Ephesians 6:10–13**

# 4

# The Tactics of Terror

I ONCE HEARD OF A MENTAL HOSPITAL that had devised an unusual test to determine when patients were ready to go back into the world. They brought candidates for release into a room where a tap was turned on, sending water pouring out over the floor. Next they handed the patient a mop and told him to mop up the water. If the patient had a firm enough grasp of reality to turn off the tap before mopping up the water, he was ready to go out into society. But if he started mopping up the water without turning off the tap, they knew that more treatment was needed.

While you and I would never miss such an obvious step as shutting off the tap before mopping the floor, the fact is that many Christians live their lives in a way that is—from a spiritual point of view—equally absurd. Each of us as Christians have been given the mop of God's truth and we have been told to use it to help mop up the evil in the world around us. But we can only be useful in mopping up the evil around us if we first have enough sense to shut off the flow of evil that pours into our own hearts from the world rulers of this present darkness.

That is exactly what the apostle Paul urges in Ephesians 6:10–13. We can be of no possible help in solving the moral, social, and spiritual problems of the world as long as we remain part of the problem. This whole passage is designed to awaken us and call our attention to the need for understanding the nature of our problem. As we have seen, it is through the channels that the Bible calls "the world" and "the flesh" that the devil makes his indirect and most insidious attack upon human life.

"The world" is human society, along with its prevailing false values, amorality and immorality, godlessness and atheism, hedonism, paganism, New Ageism, and other deceptive ideas and isms. "The world" brutally demands our conformity to its false values and ideas, and mercilessly punishes those who refuse to conform. That is why, down through the centuries and right into the present day, "the world" has practiced persecution and intimidation against Christians—because when Christians truly practice their faith and preach the gospel, the world and its false values stand exposed and condemned.

"The flesh" is that urge within us toward total autonomy and rebellion, toward being our own little gods—accountable to no one, responsible to no one, obeying no one, respecting no one, and running our own little worlds to suit ourselves. It is that continual tug of self-centeredness and selfishness within each of us that keeps us from being completely His.

As you can clearly see, this struggle against the influences of "the world" and "the flesh" is not something merely theoretical or remote from our experience. It is a battle in which we are all engaged every moment of our lives because "the world," the outer arena of battle, is always around us while "the flesh," the inner arena of battle, is always within us. We cannot escape "the world," nor can we run away from "the flesh." We must always begin our battle right at the point where we are.

John F. Kennedy, the 35th president of the United States, was a commissioned naval officer during World War II. In August 1943, the patrol torpedo boat he commanded, PT 109, was rammed and sunk by an enemy destroyer near the Japanese-held Solomon Islands. Kennedy and a fellow officer swam from one enemy-occupied island to the next until they found some friendly islanders who helped them get a message to U.S. forces. Years later, Kennedy was regarded as a war hero. His response: "It was involuntary. They sank my boat."

So it is with us. We don't have to volunteer to find ourselves in the middle of a war. It's involuntary. The war has already come to us. It is raging all around us, through the channel of "the world." And it is raging within us, through the channel of "the flesh."

You might be thinking, "That doesn't seem right at all! I thought that when you became a Christian, Jesus would set you free from the kingdom of Satan so that the devil could no longer touch you! I thought that conversion would take you *out* of the battle, not thrust you deeper *into* the conflict!" If that is your concept of the Christian life, you couldn't be more wrong! When you become a Christian, that's when the battle *really* begins!

## Miserable Christians

Certainly, it is true that the devil can never totally defeat a Christian. Those who are genuinely the Lord's, who have come into a saving relationship with Jesus Christ, have been delivered from total defeat. The devil can never get us back into the position of unconscious control he once exercised over us, as he does over the rest of the world. But the devil *can* demoralize the Christian. He can frighten us and make us miserable. He can blunt our effectiveness and make us feel weak and unfruitful for God. Even though we are ultimately victorious through Christ, it is at times possible to be more miserable as a Christian than you ever were before.

The devil has a special reason for wanting to make Christians feel defeated—because a demoralized Christian is a Christian whose effectiveness has been diminished. The unredeemed worldlings are no problem to him—they are already in his grasp. Let them try to solve the problems of their lives and the world through legislation, education, and a change of environment—none of that bothers the devil in the least. He is quite content to let them go on rearranging the pieces of the puzzle without ever solving it. But the presence of every Christian in the world bothers the devil greatly. Why? Because each Christian is a potential threat to the solidarity of the devil's kingdom, to his rule over the rest of mankind—and that is why the devil focuses special attention on us and seeks to hinder and discourage us.

When a Christian lives in obedience to the will of God, he threatens Satan's rule on earth. Every effective Christian is a potential door of escape, helping worldlings to move out of the devil's realm of darkness and into God's realm of eternal light. Every Christian who lives a life that is yielded to God and resistant to the schemes of the devil is a corridor of liberty, a center of light, dispelling one more patch of darkness and ignorance from the world around him.

The devil cannot allow people to escape from his dominion, so he is especially vicious and persistent in his attacks upon Christians. He marshals all his forces against us in order to discourage and dishearten us, so that we will not be effective and useful to God. Sometimes the devil attacks us as "a roaring lion," clawing at us through catastrophic circumstances in order to knock us off our feet and keep us from standing for God. At other times he comes as "an angel of light," a seductive and alluring temptation, offering us some attractive lure that seems so right—yet which has a deadly, poisonous trap hidden within.

To be sure, Satan will assume direct control of a human life whenever he can, producing an Adolf Hitler or a Charles Manson—demonic men, motivated by strange and unexplainable passions. Sometimes the devil assails us through "the world" with its intimidating pressure to conform, to not be different, to go with the flow lest we be ostracized and thought of as "fanatics" or "religious extremists."

But most often the devil comes in disguise, through the channel of "the flesh"—our inner selves—with silken, subtle, suggestive schemes. That is the avenue of satanic attack the apostle Paul warns us most strenuously about: the subtle schemes of the devil.

## The original extremist

According to the Bible, "the flesh," in this symbolic sense, is identified with the body that ultimately dies. Paul says, "But if Christ is in you, your body is dead because of sin, yet your spirit is alive because of righteousness" (Romans 8:10). Notice that Paul doesn't say "your body is growing old and dying," as we would say. No, he says the body is already dead. He looks to the end of our physical lives and says that it is as good as dead already.

In this temporary state we live in prior to our resurrection, the body is the seat of sin or "the flesh"—this evil principle of self-centeredness within each of us. Therefore "the flesh" is going to be with us for life. We may as well face that. We are never going to get away from it. We shall never escape it until that wonderful day of the resurrection from the dead.

But the body, soul, and spirit of man are inextricably tied together. No one can understand this. Where does your soul live in your body? Do you know? No, but you know that you have a soul, even though no one can locate it in the body. The relationship between the body, soul, and spirit is beyond our comprehension. But because they are so inextricably tied together, "the flesh," linked to the body, touches the whole person.

This is an important concept to understand. This means that the devil can influence us in the body, in the soul, and in the spirit. He has access to the whole person through the channel of "the flesh." Put another way: We are subject to the influence of these world rulers of this present darkness through our mind, our feelings, and our actions—through our intelligence, our emotions, and our will. We need to see how this works.

Through the channel of the mind—the intellect—the devil makes his appeal to human pride. Through the channel of the emotions, the devil works on human fears and passions. In the realm of our actions, our behavior, the things we choose to do and say, the devil makes his appeal to pleasure, since we are essentially sensuous beings.

See how accurately this concept is illustrated by the story of Eve in the Garden of Eden. We are told that when she saw that the fruit was good for food—it offered the pleasant sensation of eating (the appeal to the body); and it was a delight to the eyes, awakening within her a sense of beauty (the appeal to the emotions); and when she saw that it was desired to make one wise (the appeal to the pride of mind, the appeal to intelligence, and the love of wisdom and knowledge), she took it and ate.

These are simply the channels by which human beings are moved, whether for good or for ill. This is the way men and women are. Both God and the devil appeal to us and seek to move us through these channels: the emotion (the heart); the mind (the intelligence); and the will (the power to choose).

You may say, "If the devil and God both move us by the same channels, what is the difference?" The difference is simply this: The devil moves to create an imbalance, an eccentricity. The devil is the original extremist. God moves, however, toward balance, harmony, and beauty. The difference is not how they work, but the direction in which they move.

## A Sanity of Balance

The greatness of the gospel is in its appeal to the entirety of our humanity, to our whole being, body, soul, and spirit, and to the whole of life. It is this fact that reveals the divine origin of the gospel so clearly. The gospel of Jesus Christ touches and explains all of history. It has a clear and consistent worldview, and it provides a framework for every science, every endeavor to investigate reality, and every effort to understand and make sense of all the events of history.

The gospel is not content simply to treat the symptoms of the human condition. It offers a radical solution to our fundamental problem. We often come to Christ asking him to resolve some immediate difficulty in which we find ourselves, like a man with cancer going to a doctor and saying, "I have a rash on my arm. Oh, yes, I do have cancer—but don't bother with that. Just treat the rash and I'll be on my way." No doctor worthy of his medical degree would honor such a request—and neither does the Great Physician, Jesus Christ.

The Lord does not simply treat our symptoms and stop there. He knows us better than we know ourselves, and He knows that if He merely solves this small problem here or that difficulty there, He has only touched the surface of our lives. The rest of our lives, the core of our lives, will remain diseased and dying. So, in His gospel, Jesus makes His appeal and applies His power to the wholeness of our humanity and to the wholeness of our lives. His goal is to confront the eccentricity and imbalance that sin and the devil produce in our lives, and to bring us into a sanity of balance.

You can see this wonderful sanity in the life of our Lord. Read the Gospel accounts and you are instantly impressed by the marvelous balance in the personality of the Lord Jesus, and by the perfect poise He exhibits in every circumstance. His words challenge and confound the greatest thinkers of His time, and they listen to Him with astonishment at His insight and wisdom. "No man ever spoke like this man!" is their awed response—and, of course, they are exactly right. There never was another Man like Jesus Christ.

But Jesus is not all intellect, making His appeal to the philosopher and thinker alone. As you read the Gospel account, you see that He is also warmly human, a Man with an unmatched depth of compassion and human concern. He laughs, He weeps, He touches lives, He awakens the emotions and wonder of those around Him, He attracts people to Himself, He displays a supernatural magnetism and warmth. He is not content merely to feel certain emotions nor to merely communicate great truths. Rather, the beautiful balance of His personality is expressed in His practical deeds, in His actions—in the unforgettable, undeniable events like the healings, the raising of the dead, the confrontation of evil and hypocrisy, the sacrifice upon the cross, and the resounding miracle of the resurrection.

What's more, this wonderful sanity of balance that we see in the personality of our Lord Jesus Christ is also evidenced throughout the Bible. In every book, on every page of Scripture, we see that the whole man is ministered to: the needs of the soul, of the body, and of the spirit—all kept in a delicate equilibrium with nothing out of balance.

Everything is in harmony—the mind, the heart, and the will are all moved together. When God gets hold of a human life, He touches every part of that life. Anything less is an incomplete message, a mere fragment.

I am indebted to Dr. Martin Lloyd-Jones for pointing out that this sanity of balance is beautifully expressed in one of the great hymns of our faith, "When I Survey The Wondrous Cross" by Isaac Watts:

> When I survey the wondrous cross,
> On which the Prince of Glory died . . .

Notice the depth of meaning in these words: My *mind* is engaged when I think about the cross, when I give intelligent consideration to what it means, when I think of all that was involved in that supreme hour when Jesus hung between heaven and earth! The cross captures the human dimension of the intellect.

And then, another dimension of our humanity is touched by the next few lines of the hymn:

> My richest gain I count but loss,
> And pour contempt on all my pride.

My *emotions* are engaged when I think about the cross. I am moved to both grief and joy when I think of what the cross cost the Lord—and how the cross has enriched and rescued me. Anyone who can talk about the cross of Christ without being emotionally moved has not really understood the truth. The truth of the cross is designed to reach the heart, to move us and involve us at the level of our feelings. And this hymn goes on to probe our emotional response to Christ and the cross in the next lines:

> Were the whole realm of nature mine,
> That were a present far too small . . .

Here, compressed into an economy of words, is a sense of the grandeur of the work of the cross, the extent of it, and the glory of it.

> Love so amazing, so divine
> Demands my soul, my life, my all.

Love does what? It *demands*! My *will* is engaged when I think about the cross. In the words of this hymn, I find a compelling call to action.

In his baptized imagination and poetic soul, Isaac Watts understood that the appeal of the gospel is to the entire span of our humanity, in all of our human dimensions. The whole human being—mind, emotions, and will—is totally engaged by the cross of Jesus Christ. That is how God works!

He is thorough. He is balanced. And He calls each of us to this same sanity of balance.

## Grotesque caricatures

Now let's contrast the wonderful balance of our Lord with the actions of the devil. What does the devil try to produce in our lives? He tries to create imbalance! He works overtime to enlarge one element of human nature at the expense of the others. He pushes us toward extremes, and tries to turn us into people who are characterized by only one thing. Instead of whole, balanced persons, we are grotesque caricatures of what God created us to be.

There are many who actually take pride in emphasizing one part of their being above everything else. There are the intellectuals—we call them "eggheads" or "brains." They say there is nothing important in life but the mind, the ability to reason, and they give themselves over completely to the development of that one area of life. As a result, they are so absentminded, so impractical, so emotionless and arid in their personalities that we can hardly live with them! Because they are out of balance, we call them "eccentric."

Then there are the emotional people, those who say, "Oh, don't talk to me about intellectual things or practical matters. I'm a free spirit! I want to experience life! I want to feel!" These people are always living in their momentary emotions. They are led about by their feelings. They do not make careful, thoughtful decisions based on biblical principles or facts or information. They simply do whatever "feels good" or "feels right" at the moment—and as a result, they create enormous chaos for themselves and the people around them. The world has become increasingly filled with people who believe that feelings are all that matter. Rarely, anymore, do you hear people say, "What do you *think* about this or that?" Usually, people today ask, "How do you *feel* about it?"

Some feelings-oriented people are given to intense, obsessive self-examination. They marinate themselves in their own emotions, and are narcissistically introspective, endlessly examining themselves. Of course, there is nothing wrong with self-examination—kept in balance with a focus on God and on others, a certain amount of inward focus is very much a part of the Christian life. But some people never look anywhere *but* within! They are constantly looking at themselves, examining themselves, thinking about themselves, over-dramatizing themselves, talking about themselves, psychoanalyzing themselves, obsessing over themselves. As a result, they are so self-absorbed, egocentric, and emotional that we can hardly stand to be around them!

Then, of course, there are those who say, "I have no patience with intellectualism or emotionalism. I believe in being practical. I believe in action." We call such people "hard-headed pragmatists" or "do-ers." They are concerned only with deeds, accomplishments, actions, and results. They don't ask, "What do you think?" They don't ask, "How do you feel?" They ask, "What do you do?" They ask, "What have you accomplished?" They ask, "What's the practical use or benefit of this?"

These are three personality extremes—the intellectual, the emotionalist, and the pragmatist. All three of these extremes are wrong. They are unbalanced. God did not create human beings to be extremists. He created us to be balanced, to exhibit a rich and well-integrated blend of human intellect, emotion, and will. It is not God who produces these extremes in us, but the devil. The devil takes each of these facets of our humanity (which God designed to be used as human assets and strengths), and he prods us toward an unhealthy imbalance and eccentricity.

Take the realm of the mind, for instance. One of the schemes of the devil is to tempt people to exalt reason to the exclusion of faith. Faith is a function of the will, of the soul. That is why faith is the most human characteristic of humanity. It is that element of our humanity which is our basic motivator. That is why everyone can exercise faith. You are not human, you are not even alive, if you cannot exercise faith.

But the devil tries to move from a balance in this area by appealing to our pride. We love to think of ourselves as rational, intellectual beings who have a logical reason for all our ideas, beliefs, and actions. But this exaltation of reason opens the door to error and arrogant self-deception. We delude ourselves into thinking that we are motivated by logic, when in fact we are generally motivated by emotions, desires, and dimly understood drives—then we use our intellect to come up with pseudo-logical, self-deceptive rationales to justify our illogical, emotional decisions!

One of the great examples of this, which we often hear these days, is the worldly teaching that the Bible is a primitive book for a primitive age, that biblical truth and morality are "irrelevant in today's world," that all truly "enlightened," "educated," "modern," or even "post-modern" people know that the Bible is just a collection of outdated stories, fanciful myths, and out-of-date moral concepts. Secure in our intellectual smugness, we know that the Bible cannot be believed as a historical record, nor relied upon as a moral guide. Not only are we free to ignore *biblical* truth, but we don't need to believe in *any* concept of truth. We are free to invent our own reality, our own truth, our own morality, our own worldview, without some deity looking over our shoulder, telling us what is right and wrong.

The same people who tell us that the Bible is no longer relevant and trustworthy never stop to ponder the fact that the further our society moves away from the teaching of Scripture, the more debased, corrupt, and cruel humanity becomes. As the world has moved away from belief in God and the Bible, we have seen a corresponding rise in crime, political corruption, teen pregnancies, teen suicides, divorce, fatherless children, disrespect for marriage, single-parent families, abortion, pornography, drug abuse, alcoholism, racism, plus a general decline in personal integrity, responsibility, decency, and civility. The worse the world gets, the more people apply the "solutions" that created the problems in the first place—and that is why there is a spiraling upward of social ills and a spiraling downward of morality and decency in the world.

There is an active effort in our society today to erase the image of God as a loving heavenly Father. It began as an effort to devalue God's image by picturing Him disrespectfully as "the Old Man in the Sky" or "the Man Upstairs." It has gone so far today that even many churches and denominations now picture God not as a Father, but as a "politically correct" (and hence, biblically incorrect!) gender-neutral "heavenly Parent" or even a "heavenly Mother" or pseudo-goddess. The gender politics of the radical feminist movement have successfully infected the church, seeking to destroy the positive image of fatherhood and manhood in general, and the image of the heavenly fatherhood of God in particular.

If you want to be a truly "enlightened" and "contemporary" thinker today, you must not embrace the "patriarchal" concept of God the Father. No, you must view God in a more vague and meaningless way. You must view God not as a person, but as a "force" or as a "universal principle" or as "the ground of all being." This theme has been offered as if it were a revolutionary advance in theological thinking. It is, in fact, nothing but an ancient pagan heresy.

We see echoes of our own age in the story of Paul's journey to the center of intellectualism in his day—the city of Athens. As he walked around the city, he found evidences of a superstitious, ignorant, and pagan faith everywhere he went. He even found an altar dedicated "TO AN UNKNOWN GOD." Then he went to Mars Hill and gave a speech to the Athenian intellectual elite. He said to them:

> What you worship as something unknown I am going to proclaim to you.
>
> The God who made the world and everything in it is the Lord of heaven and earth and does not live in temples built by hands. And he is not served by human hands, as if he needed anything, because he himself gives all men life and breath and everything else. . . . For in him we live and move and have our being. As some of your own poets have said, "We are his offspring" (Acts 17:23–25, 28).

Paul is saying, in other words, "Look, even you as pagans are intelligent enough to know that God does not dwell in temples made of stone. How could the Creator of the universe be contained by such a paltry man-made dwelling place? Even your own Greek poets recognize the fact that God is not far from any one of us, for in Him we live and move and have our being. You already know that much about God—now I'm going to give you the complete, biblical revelation, so that you will know exactly who God is!"

Primitive faith is the simplest level of faith, and we see such primitive, uninformed, ignorant, searching, groping faith among the intellectual elite of Mars Hill, and with many of today's nonspecific, nonorganized faiths, such as the New Age movement. Many New Agers believe in a concept they call "God" but they are apathetic or actively hostile toward faith in Jesus Christ. Like the Athenians, they worship an unknown God, and they do so in ignorance. It is the devil's plan to keep such people in their ignorance, always searching and never finding the truth that is right in front of their eyes.

We also see primitive, simple faith in the recovery movement founded by Alcoholics Anonymous. Many in the recovery movement say the Lord's Prayer and believe in a "higher power" but do not recognize Jesus Christ as their "higher power." This is not a criticism of those who are at this searching, groping stage—there are many Christians today whose first introduction to God was in the form of this vague "higher power." As they grew in their understanding and dependence upon God for their sobriety, Jesus gradually revealed Himself to them. In time, they became not merely followers of a shadowy "higher power," but followers of the risen Lord and Savior, Jesus Christ.

But there are also many in the recovery movement who never move beyond primitive faith. There are even some who claim a pagan deity, a New Age concept, or some other substitute deity as their "higher power." Though the recovery movement has accomplished much good and has saved many people from alcoholism and other destructive habits, the devil will use anything to accomplish his purposes. It is part of his strategy to keep people locked in a primitive faith, never moving on to a more mature faith in Jesus Christ. The devil will frequently keep people in their primitive faith by appealing to human pride, planting such ideas in their minds as:

"I'm too sophisticated for old-fashioned, Bible-thumping, organized religion." In other words, I'm intellectually superior to those ignorant fundamentalists and evangelicals who believe that outdated book full of myths and fables.

"I believe in God, but I prefer to imagine my own God. I would rather worship God in a meadow or by a running stream than in a church." In other words, I'm intellectually superior to those poor saps who waste their Sunday mornings in church when they could be sleeping or hiking in the woods.

"I don't need to read the Bible or go to church to understand God. The Bible can mean anything you want it to, and churches are just full of hypocrites." In other words, I'm so intellectually superior to everyone else that I can make up any god I want.

The devil cleverly appeals to human pride and arrogance, duping the "intellectual elite" into thinking that ancient pagan myths and heresies are really "new advances" in religious thought!

Another scheme the devil employs against us in the realm of the intellect is doubt. The devil plants his heresies and incites false teaching. False teaching always takes an extreme position—exaggerating one particular aspect of truth and blowing it out of proportion, turning some small piece of God's truth into an overblown, extreme position. The devil even uses this ploy to promote false ideas about himself. He will cause some Christians to become so focused and fanatical about the subject of the devil and demons that they lose their focus on God and His Son and His power. To such people, the message of the devil is, "Yes! I am real, I am the devil! Remember, I am a powerful, cunning adversary, so you'd better focus all your thought and energy on defeating me!" And those who are lured into this trap run the risk of falling into the clutches of superstition, occultism, and other obsessive, fear-focused practices and beliefs.

At the other extreme, the devil will lead some people—including many church people!—to become so intellectually smug that they refuse to believe in the existence of a real, personal devil. I have actually met pastors who say, "I believe in God, I believe in Jesus Christ, but I do not believe in the existence of a personal devil." And isn't that a clever ruse on the part of the devil? Isn't concealment the perfect way to trap unsuspecting prey? That's why duck hunters hide in a blind, waiting for the ducks to pass by, unaware of the double-barreled, 16-gauge death that is waiting to explode in their direction! And this is exactly what the devil does. He hides, he lays in wait, he persuades people that there is no such thing as a real, personal devil—and that is the perfect set-up for an ambush! When humanity is unbelieving and unsuspecting, then the devil is perfectly free to do exactly what he wants among us!

Among Christians, the devil will often attack in the realm of the intellect to lead us to be overly obsessed with certain points of theology. There are many Christians who pride themselves on being intense students of the Bible and systematic theology. They have studied all the great theological schools of thought. They have wandered through all the dark woods of theological differences and have climbed the icy peaks of doctrinal fine points, such as predestination and dispensationalism and prophecy and Bible numerics and on and on. God never intended that Christians should need a doctorate of divinity or a pocket calculator to understand His Word or to live out His plan for their lives. Jesus said that the faith that saves is a childlike faith, and I believe that one of the great triumphs of Satan has been his strategy of pulling people away from a simple childlike faith and leading them into endless, pointless disputes over doctrinal minutiae.

### An appeal to fear

Another wide-open window of opportunity for the devil's scheme is the realm of emotions. We live in an age which practically enshrines the emotions as a god. "Trust your feelings, Luke!" said the New Age guru Obiwan Kenobi in the science fantasy film *Star Wars*—and millions of movie-goers have been following that deceptive advice ever since!

We are used to believing our feelings. From babyhood we have been used to reacting to the way we feel and accepting the way we feel as a legitimate and accurate description of the way things are. Nothing could be more foolish! There is no more uncertain, unreliable, and unrealistic guide in life than our feelings. Feelings come and go, and most of the time they do not relate to reality at all, because they are subject to so many influences— changing circumstances, our own changing perspective, and even the hormonal and chemical changes that take place within the human body and human brain.

The devil seduces some Christians into the belief that true worship, true faith, true joy consists of constant emotionalism. These Christians must have a regular dose of handclapping, shouting, dancing, falling down, and an array of seemingly miraculous manifestations. If they don't experience these extreme emotional experiences, they feel that they are no longer experiencing the Christian life, they no longer "feel the Spirit." This can lead to a zig-zag, up-down emotionalism where the Christian alternates between feelings of religious ecstasy and feelings of abject defeat and depression. God never intended for us to live that way. He intended us to live lives of balance and equilibrium, not trusting in momentary surges of emotion, but in His rock-steady, unchanging promises and truths.

The devil will seduce others into an opposite extreme, a morbidly unhealthy view of emotion—a view which says that happiness is sinful and that joy is a mark of spiritual shallowness. Such Christians are all gloom and introspection, and the faith they practice is a stern, gray, dismal shadow of what Christianity was intended to be.

This extreme is no more godly and Christian than is extreme emotionalism. God created us as emotional beings, and He reaches us not only through our intellect and our will, but also through our emotions. The devil's scheme is to create an imbalance and to distort our emotions so that we are in one extreme or the other, so that we are either all emotion or no emotion at all! If you find yourself in these descriptions, then it is time for you to wake up and shout, "No more!" to the schemes of the devil.

Another way the devil uses human emotion to keep Christians defeated is by leading us to be ruled by our negative emotions. He preys on our thoughts and induces worry in us, making us anxious about the future, anxious about making decisions, anxious about whether or not God really loves us and whether or not we truly belong to Him. God's prescription for this form of satanic attack is found in Philippians 4:6: "Do not be anxious about anything, but in everything, by prayer and petition, with thanksgiving, present your requests to God."

Or the devil may appeal to us through our fears. He blunts our effectiveness by making us timid and afraid to move out in faith, to live boldly and speak out boldly for God, and to dare great things for God. The devil would have us shrink back, hesitate, and tremble. The devil always appeals to our fears while God always appeals to our faith. From faith comes hope and love, but the devil wants us to give way to our fears. God's prescription for this scheme of the devil is found in 1 John 4:18: "There is no fear in love. But perfect love drives out fear, because fear has to do with punishment. The one who fears is not made perfect in love." And 2 Timothy 1:7: "For God did not give us a spirit of timidity, but a spirit of power, of love and of self-discipline."

Again and again in the Gospels, Jesus told His disciples, "Don't be fearful, don't be anxious, don't be troubled." Why? Because, He said, "I am with you." Fear and anxiety are the opposite of faith, of trust, of hope, of love. When we are fearful and anxious, we are seizing the reins of our lives from God's hands. We are saying, "God, I can't trust You to do what is right in my life. I don't know if You really know best, if You really care about me, if You're really taking care of me." Fear is the failure of faith. That is exactly what the devil is after. If you give way to fear, you will soon be discouraged and defeated. If you give way to defeat, you will begin to hate and the devil will have accomplished his purposes. He has destroyed, he has ruined, he has laid waste that which God loves and desires to bless.

In the realm of our will and our behavior, the devil seeks to draw us into a continual round of new, exciting activities. He tries to push us into becoming "workaholics," never knowing peace or rest or satisfaction, always driven, always active—and often exhausted and defeated. He may even push us toward *religious* activity, being so busy working in the church and Christian groups that we never take time to follow the prescription of Psalm 46:10: "Be still, and know that I am God." We become like Martha in Luke 10. She was always busy, always doing, always preparing and cleaning and taking care of her guests—and then she became bitter and annoyed when her sister Mary was found sitting at the feet of Jesus—listening, learning, worshiping, and reveling in the presence of her Lord. It was Mary, the learner, who chose the better part, not Martha the workaholic do-er. If you see yourself as Martha right now, you need to be very careful and very much aware that you may have succumbed to one of the devil's schemes—and it is time to wake up and find the peace and balance in life that God intended you to have.

The devil will sometimes push us in a different direction of activity—he will lead us to wear a rut in the road of our lives, to dig such a deep trench of habits for ourselves that we cannot get out. We become slaves to tradition, to habit, to daily custom, to the attitude that says, "This is the way I've always done it—why change?" So we go through our lives doing the same old thing, never risking, never attempting anything new, never allowing anything to shake us out of our complacency, until we one day reach the end of our lives only to discover that we never truly lived, never truly discovered the adventure that God planned for our lives.

God never intended life to be lived in a rut. His goal for our lives is like a great bustling superhighway right through the center of life—full of action and activity, with rest stops along the way, with occasional detours and side roads, and with an ultimate and glorious destination: our eternal home. That is the road Jesus traveled and that is the road the Scriptures lead us on.

We've just made a very brief survey of this subject, the devil's attack through "the flesh." We will learn more in the pages that follow about the devil's attack through "the world," with its illusions, its allures, and its pressures to conform, its deadly message of "everybody does it." The devil gets us that way, too. That is why we have the

Scriptures, that is why the Word of God is given to us, so that we might be instructed in all the ways that the evil one seeks to destroy us. We cannot escape if we do not know where the attack is coming from.

At this point, you may be thinking, "How can I possibly hope to fend off such attacks? The devil is too clever, and his schemes are too potent for me. I can never stand alone against such an enemy." And you are quite right—you can't stand alone. The good news is that you are not alone! Remember, Paul's word to us is: "Finally, be strong in the Lord and in his mighty power. Put on the full armor of God so that you can take your stand against the devil's schemes." You see, God has made a provision for you. Only when we recognize we are weak are we truly ready to "be strong in the Lord and in his mighty power."

## Prayer

Teach me, Father, to have the humility to admit that in my own strength I am defenseless against the snares and schemes of the devil, but that in Your strength I am invincible! Lord, help me to live a life that is whole and balanced, reflecting Your sanity of balance. Grant to me a willingness to listen, to give careful, thoughtful attention to the way of victory You have provided through Jesus Christ our Lord. He was the first one to enter the battle, and He has defeated my enemy on the cross. Though I have been slow of hearing in the past, let me now hear His clear call to me. Lord, open my eyes and ears and make me attentive to Your Word.

In the name of my marvelously wise and balanced Savior, Jesus Christ, amen.

*Stand firm then, with the belt of truth buckled around your waist, with the breastplate of righteousness in place, and with your feet fitted with the readiness that comes from the gospel of peace. In addition to all this, take up the shield of faith, with which you can extinguish all the flaming arrows of the evil one. Take the helmet of salvation and the sword of the Spirit, which is the word of God.*

**Ephesians 6:14–17**

# 5

# Armed for Battle

BRITISH ADMIRAL LORD DAVID BEATTY commanded a flotilla at the Battle of Jutland during World War I. As the battle began, British and German ships engaged each other in a long-range artillery battle. It quickly became apparent that there was a major flaw in the British ships. First, a heavy cruiser, the *Lion*, was hit by an artillery barrage and quickly sunk. Next the *Indefatigable* was hit in the powder magazine, and was blown to pieces. Then the *Queen Mary* was sunk, taking a crew of 1,200 sailors straight to the bottom. Watching this destruction among the proud ships of his fleet, Admiral Beatty turned to his bridge officer and said with characteristic British restraint, "There seems to be something wrong with our ships today, Chatfield."

Though the British ships eventually turned back the German fleet, it was later discovered that there was a fatal flaw in the design of the British ships. Though they had heavily armored hulls, their wooden decks offered almost no protection against enemy long-range artillery shells that dropped almost straight down out of the sky. Only after the British began to armor their ships on top as well as on the sides did they stop losing ships to German long-range artillery.

Effective armor is a crucial element of victory in any war—including spiritual warfare. If you leave anything unprotected, the enemy will find a way to exploit that chink in your armor—and he will destroy you. In Ephesians 6, Paul calls us to "be strong in the Lord and in his mighty power." How do we do this? How do we become strong in the Lord as Paul exhorts us to? By putting on "the *full* armor of God so that you can take your stand against the devil's schemes." And note that word *full*. We cannot merely put on this or that piece of God's armor in some random or incomplete fashion. We cannot leave any part of ourselves uncovered and unprotected. We cannot give our enemy any little opening, or he will exploit that opening to his advantage.

## The armor is Christ

After instructing us to "put on the full armor of God," Paul goes on to explain in figurative language how you and I should arm ourselves for the spiritual battle:

> Stand firm then, with the belt of truth buckled around your waist, with the breastplate of righteousness in place, and with your feet fitted with the readiness that comes from the gospel of peace. In addition to all this, take up the shield of faith, with which you can extinguish all the flaming arrows of the evil one. Take the helmet of

salvation and the sword of the Spirit, which is the word
of God (Ephesians 6:14–17).

Paul uses figurative symbols to suggest a very
substantial reality. The armor he talks about is the way to
be strong in the Lord and in His mighty power. The armor,
in short, is nothing more than a symbolic description of the
Lord Himself. The armor is *Christ*—and what He is
prepared to be and to accomplish in our lives. When Paul
speaks of these various pieces of armor, he is speaking of
Christ and how we are to regard Him and lay hold of His
power as a defense against the strategies of the devil. It is
not merely Christ as He is made available to us, but Christ
as we have actually appropriated Him for our lives.

In Romans, Paul clearly declares this concept: "Rather,
clothe yourselves with the Lord Jesus Christ, and do not
think about how to gratify the desires of the sinful nature"
(Romans 13:14). And writing to his son in the faith, Paul
tells Timothy, "You then, my son, be strong in the grace that
is in Christ Jesus" (2 Timothy 2:1). That is our armor. Christ
is our defense. So we need to study this armor to learn how
to lay hold of Christ in a practical way.

General truth, I have discovered, does not help us very
much. It is easy to speak in empty generalities about
Christian living. Sometimes we pick a phrase out of
Scripture and employ it almost as an incantation or a kind
of magic defense. But that is a grossly improper use of the
Bible.

It is easy for us to glibly tell some Christian who is
struggling through a difficult time, "Christ is the answer!"
Well yes, Christ *is* the answer, but *how* is He the answer?

What does that mean in practical terms? That is what we need to know, and this is what the metaphor of armor describes in Ephesians 6. Jesus Christ is the *specific* answer—a *specific* defense against *specific* forms of satanic attack.

Before we look at the armor more precisely, there are two things we must note which are brought out in this text. First, there are two general divisions or classifications of the pieces of armor, and these are indicated by the tenses of the verbs Paul uses. The first division, covering the first three pieces of armor, is something we have already done in the past if we are Christians. The New International Version of Ephesians 6:14–15 does not bring out the verb tense as well as other versions, such as the 1901 American Standard Version:

> Stand therefore, *having* girded your loins with truth, and *having* put on the breastplate of righteousness, and *having* shod your feet with the preparation of the gospel of peace . . .

Note the word *having* which I have emphasized in this passage. This is something that has already been accomplished for us in the past, not something we need to do in the future. We already have the belt of truth and the breastplate of righteousness and the gospel of peace!

The second division, found in verses 16 and 17, includes those things which are to be put on or taken up at the present moment:

> In addition to all this, take up the shield of faith, with which you can extinguish all the flaming arrows of the

evil one. Take the helmet of salvation and the sword of
the Spirit, which is the word of God.

We are to take up these aspects of Christ—the shield of
faith, the helmet of salvation, and the sword of the Spirit—
again and again, whenever we feel the attack of Satan.

The second thing to note about this armor is the order
in which these pieces are given to us by Paul. You cannot
alter the order in any way. For example, the reason many
Christians fail to exercise the sword of the Spirit is that they
have never first put on the belt of truth. You cannot do it in
reverse order; Scripture is very precise on this point.

## The belt of truth

Now we want to look at the first three items that
constitute the first division of this armor, beginning with
the belt of truth. That is always the place to start whenever
you are under attack. Whenever you feel discouraged,
defeated, or depressed, you begin "with the belt of truth
buckled around your waist."

The officers in the Roman army wore short skirts very
much like Scottish kilts. Over them they wore a cloak or
tunic that was secured at the waist with a belt. When they
were about to enter battle, they would tuck the tunic up
under the belt so as to leave their legs free and unimpeded
for the fight. Belting one's waist (or, as many older
translations put it, "girding the loins") was always a
symbol of readiness to fight. That is why Paul mentions
this item of armor first. You cannot do battle until you have
surrounded yourself with the belt of truth.

What does this mean in practical, everyday terms? Simply this: When you are threatened by discouragement, depression, spiritual apathy and coldness, and similar moods, you fight back by remembering that you first became a Christian by surrounding yourself with truth. You remind yourself that in coming to Jesus Christ you found the truth behind all things, you found the One who is the Way, the Truth, and the Life, the secret of the universe, the final reality!

You find the truth used in that sense earlier in this same letter: "You, however, did not come to know Christ that way. Surely you heard of him and were taught in him in accordance with the truth that is in Jesus" (Ephesians 4:20–21). Jesus is the truth, He is reality, He is the key to life, "in whom are hidden all the treasures of wisdom and knowledge" (Colossians 2:3).

"Well," some would say, "how do you know that? You say you believe in Jesus, but you have accepted him as the authority without any evidence to support it. That's blind faith." But the fact is that everyone begins with an act of faith, accepting some principle or person as the final authority in life. It is either another religious leader or a principle such as the scientific method or perhaps nothing more than "what I feel is right."

The distinctive thing about Christianity is that Jesus Christ has more clearly demonstrated the right to be accepted as that authority than anyone else or any other principle. The Christian, therefore, bets his life, in a sense, that Jesus Christ is the real authority, the true revelation of things as they really are. He has objectively demonstrated it and subjectively confirmed it to you as a Christian.

## An informed faith

How did Jesus demonstrate that He was the truth? First, by what He said. Read His words and you will find them astonishing, profound, and incomparable! He gave the most insightful glimpses ever offered to human ears of what human life is all about. Even His enemies said so. No one ever saw life and truth so clearly as Jesus did. No one ever probed so deeply or put His finger so precisely upon the elements that make up human reality. You cannot read the words of Jesus without being confronted with the undeniable fact that He *spoke* the truth—and He *was* the truth.

But beyond that, Jesus demonstrated the truth by what He did. The New Testament record is an amazing account of mighty deeds and historic events. Miracles? Yes, there are evidences of the intrusion of the spiritual kingdom— that invisible realm of reality—into the visible ream. And He capped it all, of course, by showing that He had solved the one problem that is unsolvable to every other man—the problem of death. He rose from the dead! Who else has ever done anything like that? That is why I know Jesus Christ is the truth—because He solved the problem of death.

This, by the way, is why the enemies of the Scriptures fight so fiercely to destroy belief in the historical truth of these events. They want us to think it does not matter whether these events were historically true. Of course they are historically true, and of course it greatly matters, for these events demonstrate that Jesus is the truth.

But it is not only by what He said and did that we can know He is the truth. We can know by what He is now, in this present day. What has Jesus been to you? What has He been to others? Look back at your own Christian life and its beginnings. Did He deliver you? Has He set you free? Has He broken any chains in your life? Has He been your friend? Has He brought your life toward greater balance and harmony? Has he brought you a quality of life you could have never known apart from Him? Of all the men who ever lived, only Jesus has solved the problem of life and death.

A marshal in Napoleon's army was once supremely devoted to the French emperor and military leader. After this man was mortally wounded in battle, he was carried to his tent where he underwent his death-struggle. He called out the name of the man he idolized, and Napoleon came to the man's tent. The dying man's hero worship was so great that he pleaded with Napoleon to save his life. The emperor looked helplessly at the man and said, "What do you expect me to do?" The dying marshal could not believe his ears! Certainly, the emperor would not let him die! "Save me, Napoleon! Save me!" the man shrieked as the emperor turned his back and walked out of the tent. Napoleon could not help this man. There was nothing divine about Napoleon—he had no power over life and death. Only Jesus does.

Over the centuries, people have called upon other mere mortals for help—all to no avail. If you lack courage, what should you do? You could call out, "Abraham Lincoln! Help me!" But it would do no good. Lincoln was a courageous man, but he can't give you courage. If you lack wisdom, what should you do? You could call out, "Solomon! Help me!" But it would do no good. Solomon was a wise man, but he can't help you. If you lack eloquence, you could call out, "William Shakespeare! Help me!" But no help would come.

Yet for twenty centuries, men and women in desperate need have called out, "Lord Jesus Christ! Help me!" And help comes! Deliverance comes! That is how we know that Jesus is the truth.

Remember, all competing and conflicting systems and philosophies must be tested at *all* points, not at just one. Many philosophies can provide limited help and insight in this or that area. Even Karl Marx, as misguided as he was, had a few kernels of limited and fragmentary truth embedded in his godless diagnosis of human problems. But the presence of occasional partial insights and scattered nuggets of truth does not validate a system of ideas or beliefs. Truth is a complete entity. It is all or nothing. A half-truth is frequently no better than an outright lie—and is sometimes even more deceptive than a lie. That is why witnesses in our courts must swear to tell "the truth, the whole truth, and nothing but the truth"—because fragmentary truth produces deception.

Truth is reality. Truth is the sum total of the way things really are. Therefore, truth is the explanation of all things. You know you have found the truth when you find something that is wide enough and deep enough and high enough to encompass all things. That is what Jesus Christ does.

Further, ultimate reality never changes. Another mark of truth is that *true* truth never requires updating. It never needs to be modernized. If a moral or spiritual principle was true ten thousand years ago, it is still true today. If a principle is true today, it was true a hundred thousand years ago.

A man once visited his old friend, a music teacher, and said to him in that casual way people have these days, "Hey, what's the good news today?" Without saying a word, the old man walked across the room, picked up a hammer, and struck a tuning fork. As the note sounded out through the room, he said, "That is 'A.' It is 'A' today, it was 'A' five thousand years ago and it will be 'A' ten thousand years from now. The soprano upstairs sings off-key, the tenor across the hall flats his high notes, and the piano downstairs is out of tune." He struck the note again and said, "That is 'A,' my friend, and that's the good news for today!"

Jesus Christ is unchanging. He's the same yesterday, today, and forever. That is how you know you have the truth. Remember that, when you feel defeated, when you are under attack, when doubts come flooding into your mind. Remember that you are already encircled by the belt of truth. You have found the One who is the solid, unchanging Rock. The words of the hymn express this well,

> On Christ, the solid Rock, I stand—
> All other ground is sinking sand.

## The breastplate of righteousness

Now look at the second piece of armor—the breastplate of righteousness. Have you put that on? "Having put on the breastplate of righteousness"—what does that mean in practical terms? The breastplate of righteousness is nothing more nor less than your righteous standing before God through the sacrifice of Jesus on the cross. If you have accepted Christ as your Lord and Savior, then you already have the breastplate of righteousness on. You can rest secure that your heart and your emotions are perfectly guarded and adequately protected against attack.

Christians, through one circumstance or another, often lack assurance. They feel unworthy before God. They feel they are a failure in the Christian life and that God is certain to reject them, and He is no longer interested in them. As Christians, we are constantly aware of our failures and shortcomings. Growth seems to take place so slowly. The first joy of faith has faded, and people often come to doubt God's presence with them, love for them, or forgiveness of their sin. There is a nagging sense of guilt. Their conscience needles them, making them feel unhappy and miserable. They feel God blames them. This is simply a satanic attack, a crafty and devilish accusation, a lie designed to undermine what God is doing in your life.

How do you answer an attack like this? You answer by remembering that you already wear the breastplate of righteousness. In other words, you do not stand on your own merits—and you never did. You never had anything worthwhile in yourself to offer to God. You gave all that up when you came to Christ. You quit trying to be good enough to please God. You came to God the Father on the infinite merits of His Son, who died for you. It is not your own miserable, tattered righteousness that covers your heart, but the solid, impenetrable righteousness of Jesus. And His righteousness is durable enough to deflect any of the arrows of Satan's accusations.

This is why Paul begins the great eighth chapter of his letter to the Romans with the words, "Therefore, there is now no condemnation for those who are in Christ Jesus" (Romans 8:1). No condemnation! You are believing a lie if you believe that God is angry with you and that He rejects you. Remember, you stand on Christ's merits, not your own. Later in the same chapter, Paul asks,

> Who will bring any charge against those whom God has chosen? It is God who justifies. Who is he that condemns? Christ Jesus, who died—more than that, who was raised to life—is at the right hand of God and is also interceding for us. Who shall separate us from the love of Christ? (Romans 8:33–35).

This does not mean, of course, that we can continue in our sins and God will simply wink at them. If we are sincere in making Jesus the Lord of our lives, then God will see the sins that we are still prone to, and He will say, "This child of Mine has not yet learned all that I intend to teach him or her." When we sin, He deals with us as a Father, in love and patient discipline. Because Jesus covers our sins with His blood, God watches over us as a loving Father, not as an angry judge.

See how the apostle Paul used this breastplate of righteousness when he was feeling the pressure of discouragement and defeat. Have you ever thought of the emotional struggles Paul must have had? Here was a man who was reputedly small of stature, unimpressive in his personal appearance, perhaps even disfigured, according to some evidence in the Scriptures. The last thing he had was a commanding presence.

Paul's background was antiChristian, and he could never get completely away from that. He had been the most hostile, brutal persecutor the church had ever known. After his conversion to Christ, he doubtless encountered families whose loved ones he had put to death. He was often reminded by people that he was not one of the original twelve apostles, and they continually called his apostleship into question. Writing to the Corinthians about these very matters, he says of himself, "For I am the least of the apostles, and do not even deserve to be called an apostle, because I persecuted the church of God" (1 Corinthians 15:9).

What grounds for discouragement! How easy it would have been for him to say to himself, "What's the use? Here I am working my fingers to the bone, making tents and trying to preach the gospel to these people, and look at the blessing God has brought them—but they don't care! They hurl recriminations back in my face! What's the use? Why even try anymore?"

But that is not what he does. The very next verse says, "But by the grace of God I am what I am, and his grace toward me was not without effect" (1 Corinthians 15:10). Here we see Paul using the breastplate of righteousness. He says, in effect, "I don't care what I have been. I don't defend what I am. I simply say that, by the grace of God, I am what I am. What I am is what Christ has made me. I'm not standing on my own righteousness—I'm standing on His. I am accepted by grace, and my personal situation does not make any difference at all."

So Paul's heart was kept from discouragement. He reminded himself that when he became a Christian he had put on the breastplate of righteousness. He never allowed himself to be discouraged by looking back. He always looked forward, to Christ.

## A pair of stout shoes

The third piece of armor is "with your feet fitted with the readiness that comes from the gospel of peace." Shoes are essential to fighting. Imagine a soldier clad in armor from head to foot but with no shoes—a barefoot soldier! Imagine how quickly the rough ground would tear and bruise his feet. Despite the fact that he had all the other equipment he needed, he would soon be out of action. His naked feet would render him unfit to fight. But with a pair of stout shoes, plus the rest of his armor, a soldier is ready for anything.

When Paul writes "with your feet fitted with the readiness that comes from the gospel of peace," he is talking about a peace in the heart that makes you able to fight. Does that sound contradictory—a peace that readies us for war? Not at all! The best soldier is one who is at peace with his mission, who believes he fights in a just cause, who has trust in his commanders, who knows that he is well-equipped, and who believes that victory is assured. That is precisely the peace we have as we prepare to go to war against our enemy! Christ is our peace, our source of assurance and confidence as we face the battle. He is our serenity amid the raging storm of spiritual warfare.

Now notice how all three of these pieces of armor relate to one another—and notice, also, the importance of the order in which they are listed. The first piece tells us that Christ is the truth, the ultimate secret of reality. We have come home; we have touched the key to life in Jesus Christ. That is something for the mind to understand and grasp and believe.

And then what? Well, then we know Christ. We stand on His merits. We put on the breastplate of his righteousness. We come on the basis of what He has done and not what we ourselves can do. And what is the result of that? Our hearts are at peace! Paul says, "Therefore, since we have been justified through faith, we have peace with God through our Lord Jesus Christ" (Romans 5:1). We have serenity and courage—two qualities that are best summed up in a single word: *morale*. As believers, our morale is high. We are ready for anything. No ground can be too rough for Christ. Where He leads we will follow without hesitation—even if He leads us to storm the very gates of hell itself!

In the dark days of England during the blitz, while bombs rained down on London and Coventry, the situation was truly desperate. Then Winston Churchill would come on the radio and speak to the English people when their hearts were filled with defeat and discouragement. At times they would be almost ready to quit. But that one man's voice would ring out and the nation would take heart again. The morale of an entire people would be elevated and strengthened. That is what Christ does. He speaks courage and peace to our hearts.

You see, it is not a battle against people at all, is it? It is an inner fight, a battle in the realm of the thought life and attitudes. It is a battle in the realm of your outlook on the situation in which you find yourself. This is the place to start. Remember that you wear the belt of truth. Jesus Himself is the Truth, the One worth listening to. Believe Him, Christian friend, believe and trust Him! If you are a Christian at all, if you have accepted Christ as the one who explains life and solves death, then believe what He says. Act on it. That is the belt of truth.

The breastplate of righteousness protects the emotions. You do not need to be discouraged. Of course you have failed in the past. I fail, you fail, Paul failed, we all fail. The One who has come in the flesh understands all this. He knows we are going to fail, and He knows we are going to struggle. He knows it will be an up-and-down experience and a time of battles and skirmishes—and he knows we will lose some of those conflicts. But He says, "I have taken care of all that. You do not have to stand on your merits. You stand on mine. Do not be discouraged, do not be defeated, we will win! I know what I am doing, I know how to lead you, I know what circumstances you face—and I will bring you safely through them."

The third requisite is to have your feet fitted with the readiness that comes from the gospel of peace. So remember who you are and to whom you belong. Remember, you belong to Christ's family. The Scriptures say that He is not ashamed to call us brothers. God is not ashamed to be called our Father. Be strong in *His* strength and for *His* sake.

By having these three pieces of armor on, the battle is almost won. You will be properly equipped for overcoming evil if you start with this first division of armor.

## Prayer

Father, make these words clear, plain, practical, and helpful to me. May they meet me right where I am and help me right in the conflict in which I am engaged. May my heart be lifted up by the awareness that the One who is in me is adequate for all things—even the challenge of spiritual warfare. Remind me of the belt of truth, the breastplate of righteousness, and the shoes of Your readiness through the gospel of peace. Thank You that I am already well-defended and ready for battle!

In the name of Jesus, the One who has armed me, and who defends my heart with His righteousness, amen.

*In addition to all this, take up the shield of faith, with which you can extinguish all the flaming arrows of the evil one.*

**Ephesians 6:16**

# 6

# Resisting the Devil

A MAN NAMED THOMAS became a monk, joined a monastery, and took a vow of silence. The only exception to the vow was that, once every ten years, monks were allowed to make one statement—then the silence must resume for another decade. After his first ten years in the monastery, Thomas was called into the study of his superior, who said, "Brother Thomas, do you have anything to say?"

"The food is bad," the monk replied. Then he went back to his duties.

A decade passed. Again, Thomas was summoned to the study of his superior. "Brother Thomas," said the superior, "do you have anything to say?"

"The bed is hard," the monk replied. Then he returned to his chores.

Another decade passed. Again, Thomas was called in before his superior. "Brother Thomas," said the superior, "do you have anything to say?"

"I quit," the monk replied.

The superior frowned. "I'm not surprised. You've done nothing but complain ever since you got here!"

Friend in Christ, there is nothing that more clearly indicates that we have succumbed to the schemes of the devil than to complain about our lot in life. Again and again, the Word of God shows that the mark of a Christian who has learned how to *be* a Christian is that he rejoices in everything and gives thanks in all things.

Understand, this does not mean that God expects us to *enjoy* every circumstance in our lives! Nor does it mean that we should merely *pretend* to rejoice in everything. There is nothing as ghastly as the forced smile people put on and the superficial attitude they assume in the midst of difficulties because they think this is what a Christian ought to do. The truth of Scripture is that it is genuinely possible to rejoice even through tears and pain—and there is nothing that more surely indicates that we have failed to understand what it means to be a Christian than a whining, complaining, self-pitying attitude toward what happens to us in life.

Do not be surprised at the devil's attack. Of course he attacks! That is his character. That is his nature. Do not complain that you are being treated unfairly. That is the nature of life—struggle, warfare, and satanic attack.

Furthermore, God *allows* the devil to attack. This is the clear revelation of Scripture. God permits these attacks because, for one thing, we need them. We never would develop or grow properly if we were not attacked in this manner—and this is what ultimately accomplishes God's will for our lives.

The whole outworking of God's eternal plan could never be brought to pass were it not that God permits the devil to operate within his limited sphere of activity. Let us never forget that. God allows these things to happen, and all the writers of Scripture agree on this. Peter says, "Dear friends, do not be surprised at the painful trial you are suffering, as though something strange were happening to you" (1 Peter 4:12). And the Lord Jesus Himself said, "In this world you will have trouble." But He goes on to add, "But take heart! I have overcome the world!" (John 16:33).

But this is exactly the opposite of the way we frequently feel. When attacked, we tend to think that something most unusual is happening to us. No one has ever gone through what we are going through. No one has had to undergo the depression of spirit we feel. But Paul says, "No temptation has seized you except what is common to man. And God is faithful; he will not let you be tempted beyond what you can bear" (1 Corinthians 10:13). So stop complaining about what happens. It is God's will for you. Let us face that fact.

And instead of a fretful, peevish, whining attitude, let us do what the Word of God says to do when these things occur: "Put on the full armor of God so that you can take your stand against the devil's schemes." There is no other way to handle the devil's attacks. There is no other solution to these basic human problems.

## Flaming arrows

Remember, however, as we saw in the previous chapter, we must put on our armor in the right order. We start with the belt of truth; then the breastplate of righteousness; then we shoe our feet with the readiness of the gospel of peace.

It is a mistake to start with peace. Yet that is the error most of us instantly fall into. When troubled or upset, when attacks come, our tendency is to first try to put our hearts at peace. That is a big mistake! Don't try to conjure up some kind of feeling of peace within—if you do, you will succeed only in upsetting yourself even more! So start with truth. Work your way through truth, then righteousness—and as a result, you will achieve peace. That is the proper order of the armor of God.

In practical terms, here is how it works: When attacks come, go to the truth of God—to the Word of God and to Jesus, who is Truth personified. Then focus on the righteousness of God, which you have received through the sacrifice of Jesus Christ upon the cross. As you respond to the devil's attacks with the belt of truth and the breastplate of righteousness, you will realize that God's peace is already upon you, like a comfortable, protective pair of shoes, so that you are prepared and at peace for the battle.

Now let us take a closer look at this battle. If we remind ourselves of these great truths, they ought to set our hearts at rest. But we all know that even though these truths often *will* set our hearts at rest, there are times when they do not. We are still depressed and filled with doubts.

Perhaps there is no good reason for us to feel this way. We may wake up in a blue mood even though we were happy when we went to bed the night before. There may be a simple explanation for our depression—a chemical or hormonal imbalance in the body can often cause such problems. So can poor nutrition, physical stress, illness, and lack of sleep. But at times there is really no good reason we can find for our depression—yet we still feel depressed.

Well, what is happening? We are experiencing what Paul calls "the flaming arrows of the evil one." These stratagems of Satan come to us in various forms. Sometimes they are evil thoughts and imaginations that intrude suddenly upon our thinking, often at the most incongruous times. We may be reading the Bible; we may be bowed in prayer; we may be thinking about something else entirely when all of a sudden, an ugly or lewd thought flashes into our mind. What is this? It's one of the flaming arrows of the evil one! We ought to recognize it as such.

Sometimes these arrows come as doubts and even blasphemies—sudden feelings that perhaps this business of Christianity is nothing after all but a fanciful dream.

Perhaps we feel that it can all be explained psychologically or by the suggestion that Jesus Christ was a victim of self-delusion. Perhaps the world is not the way we have been taught to believe it is, and things are not the way the Bible says. You have doubtless experienced these times of doubt. All Christians have had this sudden feeling that perhaps our Christian worldview is nothing but a hopeless fantasy. Again, these fiery arrows may come in the form of surges of unreasoning anger or hate, or sudden fears and anxieties, or just vague, fleeting sensations that things are all wrong. We cannot seem to shake them off.

So where do these fiery arrows come from?

## The devil's whispers

No matter what form they take, these fiery arrows of doubt, temptation, evil thoughts, and the like always arise from the same source. They are the fiery arrows of the wicked one. We are the biggest fools on earth if we do not see them in that light and deal with them as such. The devil's fiery arrows always have two characteristics: (1)

*These arrows seem to arise out of our own thoughts, from our own inner selves—and we are shocked and horrified that we can think such thoughts.*

But these flaming arrows don't come from our own minds. This attack is actually the devil whispering to us, influencing us. Though we may ignorantly blame ourselves, the devil is the enemy, and this is his scheme to undermine and discourage us. He wants us to blame ourselves and live in shame rather than victory. He wants us to doubt our faith or our position as children of the living God. He wants to plant a doubt in our minds, so that we will think, "I must have already lost my faith or I wouldn't think such things! What's wrong with me? How can I be a Christian and even have such thoughts?"

So we try to repress the thought and push it down and deny it—but it is still there, lurking underneath, and we feel dishonest and hypocritical because we are not even willing to look at it and face it. This takes its toll on us in the form of mental tension and emotional stress and a sense of spiritual defeat. That is the devil's goal. That is his victory.

We often feel uncertain and confused because we are convinced that the opposite of faith is doubt. We think that if we have doubts, then we cannot have faith—and if we have faith, we do not have doubts. We fail to recognize that this is merely another lie of the devil.

The next characteristic of the devil's attack is: (2) *Doubts always come as an attack upon our position in Christ—they attack His place in our lives as the truth, our righteousness, and our peace.* These arrows are always an insinuation of doubt about those matters. They are an attack upon those areas of our faith.

This has always been the strategy of the devil. He said to Eve in the garden, "Did God really say . . . ?" There is an implication of doubt that he plants in Eve's mind. And when the devil tempted Jesus in the wilderness, he said, "*If* You are really the Son of God, then turn these stones into bread." *IF!* Here again is an insinuation that these things are not true. This is the way the devil raises doubts, creates guilt, and leads people astray. These are the attacks—the flaming arrows—of the evil one.

## Quenching the fiery arrows

Now, what are we to do? How are we to combat these attacks successfully? The apostle Paul replies: "In addition to all this, take up the shield of faith, with which you can extinguish all the flaming arrows of the evil one." Notice that he does not say "the shield of belief." We have already reminded ourselves of our belief when we have put on the belt of truth, the breastplate of righteousness, and the shoe-leather readiness of the gospel of peace. That is our belief in what Christ is to us.

But faith is more than that. This is very important to see. Faith is *acting* upon belief—belief in Christ who is to us the belt of truth, the breastplate of righteousness, and the shoes of the gospel of peace. Faith is decision, action, and resolution based on the belief we have already accepted in those three realms. Let's examine each one:

1. *Truth.* Faith is saying, "Yes, I believe Christ is the truth. He is my righteousness, He is my peace—and on that basis, I now act out my beliefs in the realm of my decisions

and behavior." Faith is working out the implications of belief. Believing is generalizing. Faith is particularizing. By faith, we take the general truth and apply it to the specific situation. We say, "Because I believe this is true, these actions must follow." That is the shield of faith.

Have you learned how to take the shield of faith when doubts come? Do you say, "Christ is the truth. He is the basic revelation of reality. He has demonstrated the truth. *As a result of my belief in the truth*, I cannot accept the thought that Christianity is a hoax. I have committed myself to Christ because I have been persuaded that He has demonstrated truth fully. I stand on that ground. *As a result of my belief in the truth*, I must reject this insinuation from the devil."

Do you reason from the premise that Christ is the truth? Is this the way you think it through? Our problem is that we have become so accustomed to believing our feelings as though they were facts, we never examine and question those feelings. We never take them and look at them and ask, "Is this true?" We simply say, "I feel this way, so it must be true." This is why so many Christians are constantly defeated—they accept their feelings as facts. Instead, we must accept God's truth as fact, and regard our feelings as unreliable, because feelings come and go.

2. *Righteousness*. Instead of operating on the basis of our feelings, we are to operate on the premise that says, "Christ is my righteousness. I am linked with Him. I am one with Him. His life is my life and my life is His life. Because He and I are linked together, these evil thoughts cannot possibly be my thoughts. They are not my thoughts at all. They are thoughts that come because of another outside

force. It is the devil trying to undermine and defeat me. I do not want these thoughts, so I reject them. They are the spawn of the devil, and I order them back to where they came from and where they belong!"

Using the shield of faith means refusing to feel condemned, ashamed, or guilty. It means that instead of marinating in self-hate, we bask in God's love. We operate on the fact, as stated in God's Word, that nothing can ever separate us from the love of Christ. We say, "I believe in the fact of God's love, not in the lie of the devil." Doubts and satanic accusations cannot co-exist with the glowing reality of God's love in our lives. We cannot entertain both thoughts at the same time. When we choose to focus and meditate on the love of God in our lives, the devil's lies and accusations have to flee from us.

3. *Peace*. We must operate on this premise: "Christ is the ground of my peace. Therefore it is His responsibility to take me through every situation. So I absolutely will not believe this fear, this sudden anxiety that grips my heart. I will not believe that it is from me. It is simply sent from the enemy to shake my confidence in Christ. It is an attempt to destroy my peace and undermine my effectiveness for God. Christ is my peace, and He is able to sustain me, even through bouts of unsettling emotions and thoughts that are sent to me as fiery arrows from the enemy."

## Proof of faith's reality

The process we have just examined is what the apostle James calls "resisting the devil." In James 4:7, he writes, "Resist the devil, and he will flee from you." This is the shield of faith. It is refusing to believe the lie that if you have doubts you cannot have faith. Understand, doubt is always an attack on faith—and that means that *the fact that you have doubts indicates that you have faith!* Faith and doubt are not opposites at all. Doubt is an *indication* of the reality of faith. Therefore reexamine the ground of your faith and reassert it. Remember that feelings are not necessarily facts at all.

James says that if you keep on resisting the devil, he will flee from you. Think of that! The devil will flee from you—you can set that nasty, crafty old serpent to flight! How? Merely by resisting the devil again and again, every time an evil thought or doubt comes back. Simply refuse to yield, refuse to give up your position. Sooner or later— inevitably!—the devil will surrender and run away. Your doubts will clear, your feelings will change, the attacks will cease, and you will be back again in the sunshine of faith and the experience of the love and joy of God.

That is what Paul is talking about when he says, "In addition to all this, take up the shield of faith, with which you can extinguish all the flaming arrows of the evil one." The shield of faith is sufficient alone. It is all you need. You do not really need the other two pieces of armor. It may sound strange to say that, but it is true. You do not need any more armor, because the shield of faith is able to quench every fiery arrow of the wicked one. If the shield of faith was all you had, it would be enough for that line of defense!

Then why are we given more? Because God never intended that we should merely be conquerors. The Bible says that we are to be *more* than conquerors (see Romans 8:37), we are to be *super*-conquerors! We are not only to win; we are to win victoriously, triumphantly, abundantly.

Remember that John said, "You, dear children, are from God and have overcome them, because the one who is in you is greater than the one who is in the world" (1 John 4:4). And the apostle Paul adds, "but where sin increased, grace increased all the more" (Romans 5:20). We are intended to do more than barely make it to heaven. We are designed to triumph, to be fearless, to be not only unconquered but unconquerable!

I think so often of these words of Rudyard Kipling, describing a mature person's response to the trials, pressures, and temptations of life:

> If you can keep your head when all about you
> > Are losing theirs and blaming it on you;
> If you can trust yourself when all men doubt you,
> > But make allowance for their doubting too;
> If you can wait and not be tired by waiting,
> > Or, being lied about, don't deal in lies,
> Or, being hated, don't give way to hating,
> > And yet don't look too good, nor talk too wise;
>
> If you can dream—and not make dreams your master;
> > If you can think—and not make thoughts your aim;
> If you can meet with Triumph and Disaster
> > And treat those two imposters just the same;
> If you can bear to hear the truth you've spoken
> > Twisted by knaves to make a trap for fools,
> Or watch the things you gave your life to broken,
> > And stoop and build 'em up with worn out tools;
>
> If you can talk with crowds and keep your virtue,
> > Or walk with kings—nor lose the common touch;

If neither foes nor loving friends can hurt you;
  If all men count with you, but none too much;
If you can fill the unforgiving minute
  With sixty seconds' worth of distance run—
Yours is the earth and everything that's in it,
  And—which is more—you'll be a man, my son!

That is a very eloquent description of life. It is exactly what the Word of God is designed to prepare us for. That is what it means to "be strong in the Lord and in his mighty power."

## Prayer

Father, help me to be a person of faith, to realize that Your Word has brought to me the truth, personified in Jesus. Let me not fling away my confidence, nor cast away my reliance upon that unshakable Word, but teach me to trust in You. Empower me to show the world that this armor—Jesus Himself—is the only armor that can keep a person standing amid the pressures and struggles of this life.

I pray in the name of the Lord Jesus, the One who is my belt, my breastplate, my shoes, my shield, amen.

*Take the helmet of salvation and the sword of the Spirit, which is the word of God.*

**Ephesians 6:17**

# 7

# Hope for Clear Heads

HISTORY REVERES THE GREAT FRENCH GENERAL and emperor, Napoleon Bonaparte, as one of the greatest conquerors of all time. He conquered nearly three-quarters of a million square miles of territory for France. Adolf Hitler—a name that has become synonymous with blood-thirsty tyranny—was also an infamous conqueror, taking over some 1.3 million square miles of territory from neighboring countries before his defeat in 1945. The great conqueror Attila the Hun was a greater conqueror than Hitler, claiming 1.4 million square miles of land at the height of his reign of terror. Cyrus the Great, Tamarlane, and Alexander the Great each conquered over 2 million square miles of territory. But the greatest conqueror of all, claiming 4.86 million square miles of land, was the ruthless Chinese warlord, Genghis Khan.

Yet God tells us that he has equipped us to accomplish greater things than any of these great conquerors of history. "In all these things," Paul tells us in Romans 8:37, "we are *more than conquerors* through him who loved us." We have nothing to fear from even such a terrible enemy as Satan, because the shield of faith alone enables us to overcome anything our enemy might throw at us. The shield of faith will extinguish all of Satan's flaming missiles of doubt, confusion, disillusionment, and fear.

Even so, God does not stop there. He has given us still *more* defensive equipment, so that we may become even *more* victorious, *more* invincible. Clad in the whole armor of God, we are *super-conquerors*, and all the conquerors who have stained the pages of history with human blood are as nothing compared with God's super-conquerors—you and me.

## I am in Christ

Before going on to a consideration of the remaining pieces of armor, I would like to suggest another perspective that may help to increase our understanding of the significance of the full armor of God. We have seen that this idea of armor is an analogy or metaphor to explain in figurative terms the truth of who Jesus is in our lives and what He wants to accomplish in our lives. But the concept of armor is also an expansion of Jesus' words to His followers, "You are in me, and I am in you" (John 14:20). That is the defense of the Christian against spiritual attack: Jesus within each of us, and each of us within Jesus.

"You are in me, and I am in you." Those are some of the simplest words in the English language—so simple, any child can understand them. They are monosyllables, yet they encompass a truth so profound that I wonder if anyone can even remotely apprehend all that is involved in these simple words.

The first three pieces of this armor that Paul describes—the belt of truth, the breastplate of righteousness, and the shoes of the gospel of peace—are a figurative way of explaining this concept Christ Himself gave to us: The Christian in Christ and Christ in the Christian. When we came to Jesus Christ and believed in him, we then were "in Christ." We had a new basis of living, because we had discovered Jesus Christ to be the ground of truth, the key to life. At conversion, we found that Jesus invites us to rest upon His righteousness, so that we no longer need to manufacture our own righteousness—an attempt that would be doomed to futility. Once we were "in Christ," the struggle to justify ourselves ended, because the righteousness of Jesus completely covered us.

In the amazing experience of the cross, God transferred our sin to Christ and transferred his righteousness to us. This is the ground of our acceptance before God and the answer to the problem of human sin, guilt, and shame from which we all suffer. It was then that we learned that Christ is our peace, the source of our sense of security, wholeness, forgiveness, and well-being.

So that is the theme of the first three pieces of armor: I am in Christ. That is why the first three pieces of armor are described by Paul not as something we need to lay hold of but something we have already received. We appropriated the first three pieces of armor at the moment of our conversion, the moment we entered a new realm—"in Christ."

## Christ is in me

Now the last three pieces of armor describe what it means for Christ to be in the Christian—Christ working in our everyday lives. These last three pieces are very practical and important to us because of the problems, trials, and difficult choices we face every day. We have already seen what it means to "take up the shield of faith, with which you can extinguish all the flaming arrows of the evil one." The reason we so often experience weakness in our lives is that we do not actually take up the shield of faith! We continually try to muddle through without the protection of our faith. We do not intelligently do what God says and apply the shield of faith. In other words, we fail to draw practical conclusions from the ground of faith that we accepted at conversion.

There are only two pieces of the armor left for us to explore—the helmet of salvation and the sword of the Spirit. These two pieces of armor go on to explain what Jesus meant when He said, "I am in you." They help us to understand what it truly means for Christ to live in the Christian.

## The helmet of salvation

Now we must examine what is meant by this phrase, "the helmet of salvation." The figure of a helmet immediately suggests to us that this is something designed to protect the mind, the intelligence, the ability to think and reason.

Earlier we saw that the breastplate was the protection of our emotional life, the heart. When you figuratively put on Christ as your breastplate of righteousness, you are assuming a position in Him that protects you from the sense of guilt and unforgiveness—the most common source of disturbance to the emotions. It is because we feel guilty that we get emotionally upset and depressed—and

God has given us the breastplate of righteousness to protect us right at this point of attack. The shoes, as we have already seen, protect us in the area of our will. The shoes of the gospel of peace (Christ is our peace) create a readiness and willingness within us. It is our motivations which are dealt with here. Christ as our peace motivates us and makes us ready to face the struggles of life.

But the helmet is designed for the head, for the intelligence, the mind. If we follow through consistently in our application of these pieces of armor, we will discover that the helmet represents something Christ is doing in us and through us in the world. This helmet can keep our thinking straight and preserve us from mental confusion and darkness.

Let me ask you this: As you look at our spiritually aimless, and morally confused world, is there anything we need more desperately than clear thinking? Is there anything more relevant to the spiritual and moral disintegration of our age than something to keep our thinking straight? Was there ever a time when human beliefs and ideas were more chaotic and anarchic than *this* moment, as we move into a new millennium? Even the intelligentsia of our times, the "best and brightest" of our age, admit to being utterly baffled by the dangerous social, political, and moral problems that confront our society.

Just think about the staggering complexity of the issues of our day—runaway crime rates, cities where criminals run free and citizens tremble in fear behind iron bars; child neglect, child abuse, and child pornography; political corruption and rampant immorality in our government; spiraling rates of teen pregnancy, single parenthood, fatherless children, and abortion; festering racial strife and gender warfare; exploding terrorism and expanding proliferation of nuclear, biological, and chemical weapons; the breakdown of the family and the rise of immorality in our homes, in the media, and on the Internet, and on and on and on! Where can it all end—but with the end of civilization itself?

The mind is simply overwhelmed by the perplexity of the problems we face. The great futurist, H. G. Wells, was in a state of extreme despair when he wrote these depressing words at the close of World War II:

> Quite apart from any bodily depression, the spectacle of evil in the world—the wanton destruction of homes, the ruthless hounding of decent folk into exile, the bombings of open cities, the cold-blooded massacres and mutilations of children and defenseless gentle folk, the rapes and filthy humiliations, and above all, the return of deliberate and organized torture, mental torment and fear, to a world from which such things had seemed well-nigh banished—all these have come near to breaking my spirit altogether.

And listen to this startling statement by George Bernard Shaw:

> The science to which I pinned my faith is bankrupt. Its counsels, which should have established the millennium, led instead directly to the suicide of Europe. I believed them once. In their name I helped to destroy the faith of millions of worshippers in the temples of a thousand creeds. And now they look at me and witness the great tragedy of an atheist who has lost his faith.

What a revealing confession of mental confusion and darkness by some of the great leaders of thought in this century! There is no protection in this chaotic world for the human mind.

## A future salvation

But the Christian has the helmet of salvation. "Well," you say, "what is that? What is this helmet, this protection, which keeps our thinking straight in the midst of a confused, chaotic world?" Paul answers: It is the *helmet of salvation.*

What does Paul mean? He is not talking about the salvation of the soul. He is not referring to salvation as regeneration or conversion. In other words, he is not looking backwards, to the moment of conversion. The first three pieces of armor do so, but the next three pieces of armor, including the helmet of salvation, look forward, not back. Paul is talking about a salvation that will be a future event. It is exactly what Paul refers to in Romans when he says, "Our salvation is nearer now than when we first believed" (Romans 13:11).

This helmet is further defined for us by the apostle in his first letter to the Thessalonians: "Since we belong to the day, let us be self-controlled, putting on faith and love as a breastplate, and the hope of salvation as a helmet" (5:8). Here, salvation is a hope, something yet in the future, something as yet not possessed or entered into fully. This future tense of salvation is described for us in a number of passages, but it is discussed very plainly in Romans:

> We know that the whole creation has been groaning as in the pains of childbirth right up to the present time.

Not only so, but we ourselves, who have the firstfruits of the Spirit, groan inwardly while as we wait eagerly for our adoption as sons, the redemption of our bodies. For in this hope we were saved. But hope that is seen is no hope at all. Who hopes for what he already has? But if we hope for what we do not yet have, we wait for it patiently (Romans 8:22–25).

What is Paul talking about? He is talking about the day of the return of Christ, the day when creation will be delivered from bondage by Christ's return to establish His kingdom. This helmet, therefore, is the recognition that all human schemes to obtain world peace and harmony are doomed to fail—but the plan of God is moving forward, right on schedule. Jesus Christ *is* coming back, and He *will* appear again, and He *will* establish His own reign in righteousness on the earth. That is the helmet of salvation which will keep your thinking straight in the hour of man's utter confusion and darkness.

The principle of God's working is declared over and over in Scripture. It is written for all to read. "No flesh," God says, "shall glory in my presence" (see 1 Corinthians 1:29 KJV). In other words, nothing that man can boast of shall contribute one iota to the true solution of the human dilemma. It is all of God. He will establish it—and there is no human wisdom, human knowledge, human psychology, nor human science that can contribute to it. According to the record of Scripture, all that humanity boasts of and places trust in shall crumble into dust. Everything that can be shaken shall be shaken, and only those things which cannot be shaken shall remain. The things that cannot be shaken are the things of God. No one shall glory in his presence.

But that isn't the whole idea. Don't stop there. If you do, you will fall into the extremism by which the devil keeps us off balance and eccentric in our thinking. God is working through these events of history, but He is working out His purposes on a basis totally different from the aims and goals of human beings. That is the helmet of salvation. We should not be taken in by the unreal and groundless expectations of the world, placing our reliance upon political solutions, social programs, or scientific advances to solve the problems of humanity. We must place our reliance on God's plan alone.

Yet, at the same time, we must not withdraw from the world and isolate ourselves from its problems. Here is where we must maintain our balance. Even though political solutions will never produce Utopia, we must exercise our rights and responsibilities as good citizens and voters to support moral, ethical, and godly government. Even though social programs will never produce Utopia, we must be involved in meeting human needs, reaching people in the depths of their pain, hunger, nakedness, imprisonment, and loss, because that is when their hearts are the most open to the ultimate solution for their problems—salvation through Jesus Christ. Even though science can never produce Utopia, we must use every modern means—from video to satellite TV to the Internet—to proclaim the truth of God's plan to a truth-starved world.

Christians are to be involved in world events—but we are involved for entirely different reasons than the worldlings are. Christians are to be involved to accomplish God's plan to reach every human heart in every corner of the world with the good news of salvation in Jesus Christ. If you can keep God's eternal plan in view at all times, it will save you from enormous heartache and fear as you read your daily newspaper. When you see the chaos in the world, you will know that even the disorder that Satan seeks to stir up in the world is being used to further God's plan and bring His kingdom one day nearer. Though we are often shocked whenever we open a newspaper or turn on CNN, God is never surprised. His plan is right on schedule.

Why are thoughtful minds like H. G. Wells and George Bernard Shaw so bewildered by what they find in life? Because they pin their hopes on fallible, unreliable human enterprises—on knowledge, education, politics, and science. As the Dean of the University of Melbourne wrote concerning H. G. Wells:

> He hailed science as a panacea for all ills and the goddess of knowledge and power. In a series of popular scientific romances he visualized the luminous *Shape of Things to Come*. In *Food of the Gods* he described a future of bigger and better men. He spoke of a planned world, of eugenics, of mechanized labor, of scientific diet and scientific education.

How much we still hear these phrases tossed about in our own day! But all human efforts to achieve Nirvana, Utopia, Shangri-La, and Heaven on Earth are doomed to fail! Such grandiose dreams are built on a cloud, a cobweb, a shimmering illusion. And when the illusion changes shape, as all illusions eventually must, their castles in the clouds come tumbling down. This has been the repeated pattern of history for twenty or more centuries—men building upon shifting, ephemeral, and temporary things instead of on the unshakable things which always remain, to which the Scriptures testify.

## Salvation is coming—*and is now at work!*

So we, as Christians, have the helmet of salvation. We have a hope for the future. We understand that God is working out His purposes and therefore we are not disturbed when human programs go wrong and everything fails. We are not surprised when all the plans and programs for human progress end up in the same old ash-heap—the New Deal and the Fair Deal, the Great Society and the New World Order. We have learned to *expect* wars and rumors of wars, right until the very end. We *expect* false teachings and false philosophies and cults and heresies to abound. We have been told that all these things will happen.

So we are not surprised, we are not panicked, we are not stampeded by events. We know that everything around us—all the ethical upheaval and moral chaos—will ultimately be resolved by God's program. We can live unafraid in a world of fear and terror because we know that God is moving in history, and nothing that happens can upset or delay His plan.

The Christian knows that wars are unavoidable, even though every effort should be made to avoid them—and that there is no contradiction in this. The Christian knows that war is madness and that nothing is really solved by war. But he knows also that we are living in a mad world, a world that is deluded by silken, subtle, satanic lies that are deliberately designed to mangle and mutilate the bodies and souls of human beings.

The world is in such a state and condition that although the Christian knows we are called to do whatever we can to prevent and relieve human suffering, the innocent and the weak *will* suffer and nothing much can be done about it at times. The blame lies squarely on the stubborn refusal of people everywhere to grapple with the true nature of the problem and accept the remedy that God's love has fully provided. The Christian knows that demonic forces can arise and possess the world from time to time, and that every human scheme to control them will ultimately fail.

God forgive us, for we have too often appeared uncaring or uninvolved in the pain and upheaval of the world. We have given the appearance of being so heavenly minded that we are of no earthly good! We have been all too willing to let the world go to hell, saying, "What do I care? I'm going to heaven!" It is time we ask God to restore within each of us a godly balance in which we care about the fate of the world without being paralyzed by fear. It is time we roll up our sleeves and do all we can to rescue the worldlings from the horrors of the future. It is time we make it clear to the people around us that while Utopia is a fraud and a fantasy, heaven is real and within their reach.

Even though we know that the world is doomed, we are not hopeless, we are not resigned, we are not fatalistic, we are not in despair. Though we have no hope in humanity, we have every hope in God. That is why we do not withdraw from life—we are fully engaged! That is why we do not retreat and build little air-tight capsules of Christianity and shut out the world—we are involved in the world! That is why we do not fight the battles of this world on the world's terms—we fight on God's terms! That is why we do not wish the world well as it goes to hell—we point the way to heaven!

The helmet of the hope of salvation not only tells us that these things are happening and will happen, but that a certain, sure salvation is coming—*and it is even now at work!* This is what we need to know. Not merely that history will ultimately come out all right in the end, but that the ending is being worked out *right now!* History is not a meaningless jumble, but a controlled pattern, and the Lord Jesus Christ is the One who directs these events. He is the Lord of history.

Moreover, as we have already seen in the Gospels, Jesus would be a formidable opponent to any who hypocritically use a cause to advance their own purposes or to mislead and defile the minds and hearts of others. As he stood before Pilate, Jesus said, "My kingdom is not of this world. If it were, my servants would fight to prevent my arrest by the Jews. But now my kingdom is from another place" (John 18:36).

In other words, "I am no threat to you, Pilate. My kingdom is not of this world. I am not involved in any political movements that seek to overthrow you. Yes, I am a king—but not in any political sense. Yes, I am involved in history—but my plan is bigger and more long-range than you can imagine. I am not merely moving the events of the government of Palestine or the government of Rome, but of the government of the entire universe, all of space and all of time."

Jesus is not a friend of this political movement nor of that political party. He is today what He has always been: the Friend of sinners.

## Hope neglected, hope abandoned, hope restored

One of the great reasons the church is so confused in this day, one of the reasons the church says so little of true significance to the world, is that it has neglected and abandoned, by and large, the hope of the coming of the Lord. There are very few sermons preached on it. There is very little said about it. There is no time given to a consideration of what this hope means and why it is set forth so frequently and so clearly in the Scriptures. Great sections of the Scriptures that deal with the hope of our Lord's return are simply ignored by Christians.

As a result, our thinking is muddled and confused. The church does not know which side to take or where to stand. It has nothing to say. At best, the church today sounds an uncertain call that fails to summon anyone to battle, and does little to encourage the heart.

God, in His Word, has called us to remind ourselves and each other of the coming of the Lord. How many times did Jesus say, "Watch and be ready for that hour." We must live daily in the hope and anticipation of that triumphant moment. The battle is not ours but the Lord's. We often think of this great struggle against the devil and his angels, against the principalities and powers, against the schemes of the devil, as though it were primarily a private fight between us and the devil. No! This battle is the Lord's!

It's true that the battle rages all around us and within us. It storms into our churches, our homes, our work places, our neighborhoods, our relationships with our fellow human beings. But when Satan's blitzkrieg assaults us, we must remind ourselves that this battle is not ours, but the Lord's. We are individual units fighting in a great army. The ultimate cause is sure and the end is certain. We do not need to be troubled by all the terrible events that go on around us and on the nightly news, nor by the struggle that rages within us. Our Lord and Commander has already won.

Though we may be hard pressed in our immediate realm in this battle, the cause is never in doubt. The end is absolutely certain; the outcome is sure. It is not ultimately a struggle between us and the devil but a struggle between Christ and Satan. Christ is always at work in human life and in society. He is at work through His body, the Christian church, to heal and to help, to love and to sympathize, until that morning without clouds dawns and the day breaks and every shadow flees from sight.

Are you frightened by world events? Then let me "reassure" you: It's going to get much worse! Jesus said men's hearts shall fail them for fear because of things that are coming to pass on the face of the earth. "Some reassurance!" you say. But it's true—the worse things get, the nearer the Lord's return. Our job is to eagerly await His return. Our job is to expect His coming and to be prepared for it. Our job is to pray and serve and obey and be ready. So the worse things get, the nearer our deliverance!

If you think it is hard to stand now, if world events throw you for a loss now, how will you stand when the darkness increases, when the cause looks hopeless, and things get very much worse? That is the hour when we must have the hope of salvation—the helmet of salvation that protects the mind. The writer of Hebrews says, "Yet at present we do not see everything subject to him. But we see Jesus, who was made a little lower than the angels, now crowned with glory and honor because he suffered death, so that by the grace of God he might taste death for everyone" (Hebrews 2:8–9). It is this hope that sustains the mind in all hours of pressure.

Here in this favored land of ours we have so much for which we can give thanks. God in His grace has granted that we might be relatively free from so much suffering and privation that we see in other countries. There are great areas of the world where faith may not be expressed openly, where the darkness is far greater than here, where the forces of wrong stride unopposed through the land, and nothing seems to stand in their way. Despite our constitutional government, there is no guarantee that the freedom we now enjoy will always be ours, and you and I may someday face the same kind of persecution we see in other lands today.

What do Christians do in those places? There is only one thing they can do: They must put on the helmet of the hope of salvation. This keeps their thinking straight. It directs them in the causes to which they give themselves. It gives them advice and counsel as to where they should put their efforts and in what they should make investments of time and money and enterprise.

The helmet of salvation can do the same for us. We need not succumb to the delusion of the world—the belief that human effort can bring about redemption, salvation, and the resolution of all human problems. How long has the world grasped at that futile dream? Read the ancient writings of the Greek philosophers and you will see that they were saying the same things and dreaming the same utopian dreams even then. As far back as human history goes, people have chased this elusive hope that some form of heaven can be worked out on earth.

But God has never said that. Consistently, throughout Scripture, He tells us that fallen man is incapable of solving his own problems. Only the hope of salvation can keep our minds and our hearts calm and undisturbed in the day of battle, in the day of darkness.

## Prayer

Father, thank You for providing me with the helmet of salvation, the hope of Your ultimate justice and ultimate peace—a hope that will be realized on the day of the Lord's return. I know that things are not nearly as bad as they could be, nor even as bad as they will be. But I thank you for the constant assurance You give to me that even when events grow worse and the days grow darker and human hearts grow colder, nothing happens that is outside of Your plan. You are never surprised or caught off-guard. The battle is Yours, not mine. Thank You for the certainty that I stand in the power of Jesus and in the strength of His might. Thank You that my hope is not in some flimsy human program or scheme, but in Your eternal purposes.

In the name of the One whose return I eagerly await, our Lord Jesus Christ, amen.

*Take the helmet of salvation, and the sword of the Spirit, which is the word of God.*

**Ephesians 6:17**

# 8

# Spiritual Swordsmanship

THE GLITTERING FLASH OF STEEL by firelight! The clash and clang of blade against blade! The sneering taunt by one swordsman to another, as two determined opponents match wits as well as swords! That is the stuff of a grand adventure story! Here, for example, is a passage from that Alexandre Dumas classic of swashbuckling adventure and swordplay, *The Three Musketeers*:

> "What is your name, my brave fellow?" said Athos.
>
> "D'Artagnan, monsieur."
>
> "Well, then, Athos, Porthos, Aramis, and D'Artagnan, forward!" cried Athos.
>
> "Come, gentlemen, have you decided?" cried Jussac. . . .

"We are about to have the honor of charging you," replied Aramis, lifting his hat with one hand and drawing his sword with the other.

"Ah! You resist, do you?" cried Jussac.

"Does that astonish you?"

And the nine combatants rushed upon each other with a fury which however did not exclude a certain degree of method. . . . D'Artagnan sprang toward Jussac himself. . . . Jussac was, as was then said, a fine blade, and had had much practice; nevertheless it required all his skill to defend himself against an adversary who, active and energetic, departed every instant from received rules, attacking him on all sides at once, and yet parrying like a man who had the greatest respect for his own epidermis.

This contest at length exhausted Jussac's patience. Furious at being held in check by one whom he had considered a boy, he became warm and began to make mistakes. D'Artagnan, who though wanting in practice had a sound theory, redoubled his agility. Jussac, anxious to put an end to this, springing forward, aimed a terrible thrust at his adversary, but the latter parried it; and while Jussac was recovering himself, glided like a serpent beneath his blade, and passed his sword through his body. Jussac fell like a dead mass.

That is fictional swordplay. But here, torn from the pages of historical fact, is a brief but thrilling passage from a timeless chronicle of the buccaneers, Howard Pyle's *Book of Pirates*:

Suddenly, the mouth of a pistol was pointing straight at the lieutenant's head. He ducked instinctively, striking upward with his cutlass as he did so. There was a stunning, deafening report almost in his ear. He struck again blindly with his cutlass. He saw the flash of a sword and flung up his guard almost instinctively, meeting the crash of the descending blade. Somebody shot from behind him, and at the same moment he saw someone else strike the pirate. Blackbeard staggered again . . . toppled and fell. The pirate lay still for a moment—then rolled over—then lay still again.

Adventure aficionados down through the centuries have been fascinated by swords and swordplay—from the sturdy broadswords of the ancient Romans and Greeks to the thin rapiers of *The Three Musketeers* to the wicked, curved cutlasses of pirates like Blackbeard. As we come to the last piece of armor Paul lists for us in Ephesians 6, we discover that this piece is "the sword of the Spirit, which is the word of God." Swordsmanship, we learn, is an essential part of the Christian life.

But the swordsmanship God calls us to in Ephesians 6:17 is not a romanticized, swashbuckling adventure of smirking villains, dashing heroes, and flashing steel. The sword of the Spirit is a practical piece of armor, designed to make us strong for the very real battle that each of us must face on a daily basis.

### The sword is Christ

We begin our study of spiritual swordsmanship by underscoring the fact that the sword of the Spirit is Christ.

Jesus Christ is our life, if we are Christians at all, and God has made His Son available in a practical, everyday way through the sayings of His word. I cannot overstress this fact. It is easy to have a vague sense of following Christ without knowing, in specific and concrete terms, what this means. That is why the Word of God has been given to us—Christian truth as a whole is more than we can handle, but the individual promises of Scripture make Christianity manageable and practical. Writing to the Colossians, Paul says,

> Let the word of Christ dwell in you richly as you teach and admonish one another with all wisdom, and as you sing psalms, hymns and spiritual songs with gratitude in your hearts to God (Colossians 3:16).

Here Paul indicates that the authority of Jesus Christ and the authority of Scripture are one and the same. There are many today who challenge that. There are many voices telling us that as Christians we must follow Christ and accept the authority of Christ, but we need not accept the authority of the Bible. But Paul answers that by calling the Scriptures "the word of Christ." You cannot separate the two.

I once attended a meeting of ministers at which we listened to a Christian professor deliver an excellent paper on "Science and the Christian Faith." After he had finished, questions were addressed to him by members of the group. One man said, "I can accept the Bible as a witness of certain men to what they thought of Jesus Christ. But you seem to go further. You have used the word 'inspired' on several occasions in your paper and that seems to suggest that in your opinion the Bible is more than the views of men, that it has divine authority. Is this true?"

The Christian professor gave a very wise answer, "My answer may sound to you very much like Sunday school propaganda, but I can only put it this way: The center of my life is Jesus Christ. I have found him to be the key to everything I desire in life. And yet I could know nothing about Christ if I did not learn it from the Bible. The Bible presents Christ and Christ defines the Bible. How can I make a distinction between the two?"

With considerable embarrassment the questioner threw up his hands and changed the subject.

The authority of Scripture is the authority of Jesus Christ—they are indivisible. To attempt to separate the two is like asking which blade of a pair of scissors is more important or which leg of a pair of pants is more necessary. We know Christ through the Bible, and we understand the Bible through the knowledge of Christ—the two cannot be separated. That is why Paul calls it "the word of Christ."

## The sayings of God

Having said that, it is important to understand clearly what Paul means—and doesn't mean—by the phrase, "the sword of the Spirit, which is the word of God." It is important to see that Paul doesn't mean the complete Bible when he says "the Word of God." There are two words that are used in the original Greek Scripture for "the Word of God." There is the familiar Greek word *logos*, which is used in the opening verse of John's Gospel, "In the beginning was the *Logos* [Word], and the *Logos* was with God, and the

*Logos* was God." Then there is another word, used less frequently, *hrema*, which is somewhat different in meaning than the first.

The word *logos* refers to the total utterance of God, the complete revelation of what God has said. The second word, *hrema*, means a specific saying of God, a passage or a verse that has special application to an immediate situation. It implies a use of the Word of God that is applied to a specific experience in our lives.

The second word, *hrema*, is the one used here. The "sword of the Spirit" is the saying of God applied to a specific situation in your life. That is the great weapon placed in the hands of the believer. Perhaps you have had some experience with this. Sometimes, when you are reading a passage of Scripture, the words seem to suddenly come alive, take on flesh and bones, and leap off the page at you. Sometimes they seem to grow eyes that follow you around everywhere you go, or develop a voice that echoes in your ears until you cannot get away from it. Perhaps you have had that experience in some moment of temptation or doubt when you were assailed by what Paul calls here "the flaming arrows of the evil one." And immediately a passage of Scripture that supplies the answer comes flashing to mind.

That passage of Scripture is God's *hrema* for you.

Or perhaps you have been asked a question that caught you off guard for a moment and you were about to say, "I don't know," when suddenly you had a moment of illumination and a word of Scripture came to mind that provided the answer. Perhaps this experience has happened while sitting in a meeting where some message has come home to your heart with an unusually powerful effect. You were greatly moved, and in that moment you made a significant and lasting decision.

That illuminating word of Scripture was God's *hrema* for you.

The *hrema*-word of God in your life is called "the sword of the Spirit" because it not only originated by the Spirit as the author of the Word but it is also recalled to your mind by the Spirit and made powerful by Him in your life. It is His specific, well-chosen answer to the attack of the devil. Like a swordsman with a trusty blade in his hand, the Spirit brings a flashing, sharp-edged, highly polished word to our mind to parry the sword-thrust of the devil.

## The only offense

Up to this point, all the pieces of armor we have examined have been defensive in nature. The belt, breastplate, shoes, helmet, and shield are all designed to protect you from attack and harm. But a sword is useful for both defense and for offense. So it is with the sword of the Spirit, the Word of God. As a sword, the Word is useful for *both* defensive and offensive purposes. It is, in fact, the only part of the armor of God that can be used for offense. It protects us for attack, in that it can be used to parry and deflect the vicious sword-strokes of the enemy—but it goes further, in that it can also be used to pierce other human hearts with the truth and to hack away and kill the lies of the devil in others besides ourselves. That is its great effect.

The Word is the only proper offensive weapon in the Christian's armory. We are to proclaim the truth. We do not need to defend the truth. We do not need to support the truth with long and extensive arguments. There is a place for that, but not in an encounter with those who disbelieve. We are called to simply proclaim and declare the truth.

As the Scripture says in Hebrews: "For the word of God is living and active. Sharper than any double-edged sword, it penetrates even to dividing soul and spirit, joints and marrow; it judges the thoughts and attitudes of the heart" (Hebrews 4:12). It cuts through the hardened armor of human arrogance, intellectual rationalization, agnosticism and atheism, sin and pride, and it homes in on the heart. The sword of the Spirit needs no defense, because it is its own defense, as well as its own offense. It is its own power supply, because it is the living and active word of Christ.

It is this offensive power of the Word that explains why the Bible is so continuously under attack. For centuries the enemies of the gospel, prompted by the devil, have tried to destroy the Bible. Sometimes this effort has been directed at completely wiping the Bible off the face of the earth. At other times, the enemies of the Bible have tried to destroy its significance through intellectual attacks or ridicule. In our own time, the primary means of attack has been to undermine its significance in the minds of people—to attack and ridicule the Bible in the media, in the arts, in schools and universities, and even in churches that practice a liberal, humanistic theology. With clever words and subtle arguments, the devil speaks through people of prominence and intelligence to blunt, twist, and disable the testimony of the Scriptures.

This does not mean that these prominent people are necessarily hypocritical. It is not that they are being deliberately and knowingly destructive. Many of them are sincerely attempting to be what they may describe as "honest to God." But notice the focus of these intelligent and subtle arguments: They are always an attempt to disprove the historical trustworthiness of the biblical record, particularly in relation to supernatural events. They cannot accept the idea that an invisible realm (which the Bible calls the kingdom of God) has invaded our commonplace realm of space and time. Such a concept is distasteful to them, so their attacks are aimed at making the Bible accounts appear incredible and unreliable, not to be taken seriously.

Many of these speakers and professors and doctors of theology claim to be Bible scholars, but they betray the Scriptures with the kiss of Judas and mislead thousands. The intent, of course, is to keep people from reading the Bible. That is the devil's principal strategy. The devil has declared war on God's Word because he knows the power of Scripture. He knows that when people are awakened to the truth of God's Word, he loses his power over their minds, hearts, and will. His aim is to keep people from seriously, thoughtfully examining the Scriptures. He knows that the Scriptures are living and powerful, and a sincere, open-minded reading of the Bible is all anyone needs to answer the attacks of the critics and scholars.

## The answer to the critics: Just read

Take, for example, the story of the first Christmas. Nothing is more basic and central to the Christian message than the story of the way the infinite Son of God became a finite baby in a manger and was welcomed with the angels' praise, a brilliant star, the coming of the shepherds, and later, the wise men. We love the simple beauty of that ancient story. It transforms the world (at least outwardly) for a brief time every year and has done so for twenty centuries.

But the false prophets of our day treat this story as if it were nothing but a myth, a pretty adornment for a holiday greeting card. There is no attempt at all to disprove the supernatural claims of the biblical story—the story is merely dismissed with a wave of the hand. Scorn is heaped upon this story as unworthy of modern intelligence. The implication is clear that any who believe in this story is in a class with those who still believe in a flat earth or in the existence of fairies.

The reason for this, of course, is that any acceptance of the biblical account as historical fact means that its implications cannot be swept aside. We must face it as an incontrovertible event that can only be explained by the biblical explanation: The lost condition of humanity has been invaded by God so that—at great cost to Himself—He could redeem humanity and set men and women free.

What is the answer to the false claims that accounts of supernatural events are merely myths? Simply this: *Read the Bible.* Read the Christmas story as told by Matthew and Luke. As you approach the familiar account with an open mind, you will see how candidly and plainly it is presented, and how uncontrived the record is. There is no attempt to garnish it or to bolster it with arguments or theological explanations. There is just the simple narrative of what happened to a couple on their way to Bethlehem, what occurred when they arrived there, and what happened in the days following. When that story is set in place in the total narrative of the Bible, you instantly see how fitting it is, how natural and believable.

From that simple story, all light is streaming, all hope is flaming, all songs are coming. Wesley captures this beautifully in his hymn,

> Late in time behold Him come,
> Offspring of a virgin's womb.
> Veiled in flesh, the Godhead see,
> Hail the incarnate Deity!
> Pleased as man with men to dwell,
> Jesus, our Emmanuel.

This simple, uncomplicated story was widely accepted and proclaimed in the first century. Along with the account of the cross and the resurrection, that story completely changed the world. No Christian in the Scripture ever denies it. No apostle ever questioned these events, nor suggested that they did not take place exactly as recorded. The stories were well known in their day.

In other words, this account reflects the inherent ability of truth, simply told, to compel belief without artificial support. As we read the account, it wins the submission of our reason, it appeals to the love of the heart, and it compels the obedience of the will. To reject it, therefore, is to violate our basic humanity. This is why John declared in a letter written toward the close of the first century that this story is one of the tests of false teachers. He declared that if someone denies the incarnation and says that Jesus did not come in the flesh, he is inspired by a wrong spirit and is an antichrist (see 1 John 4:2–3).

## The sword in action

The purpose of the Word, these "sayings of God," is to compel belief in the face of any distortion of truth. Looking back in my own life, I recall many times when the sword of the Spirit has saved me from error and delusion of one kind or another. As a young Christian, I was stopped at the edge of disobedience many times when temptation to sin seemed so logical, so reasonable, so widely practiced that I was strongly drawn by it. I was often arrested by a word I had memorized as a young Christian and which has come to me many times since: "Trust in the LORD with all your heart and lean not on your own understanding; in all your ways acknowledge him, and he will make your paths straight" (Proverbs 3:5–6).

It is so easy to think that because something looks logical to us it must be logical. But we fail to recognize the fact that we are easily deceived. We are not the rational creatures we love to think we are. There is much illusion and delusion in our world, and by ourselves we are not intelligent enough to see through these phantasms, these lies. Therefore the word comes, "Trust in the LORD with all your heart." Believe the truth as it is revealed, and "lean not on your own understanding."

Sometimes a sword of the Spirit has been placed in my hand, not before defeat but right in the midst of it, or right afterward. It has thus become the means of preventing any painful recurrences. I remember when a word from the book of James came home to me with unusual power after a very violent and nasty display of temper on my part. A verse flashed into my mind which I had read in the letter of James, "Man's anger does not bring about the righteous life that God desires" (James 1:20). That arrested me. I thought, *Here I am claiming to be interested in working the righteousness of God, and what am I doing? Losing my temper! Flaring up at someone—then thinking I am accomplishing what God sent me to do.* That verse stopped me then and has been a help ever since.

I remember another time when my heart was pierced by these words from the book of Proverbs, "Pride only breeds quarrels, but wisdom is found in those who take advice" (Proverbs 13:10). When we get involved in contention and strife with one another, it is so easy to blame the other fellow. He started it! One day a nephew of mine and my daughter were fighting, and I asked them, "Who started this?" The boy said, "She did. She hit me back." That is so like us, isn't it? But the Word says, "Pride only breeds quarrels." Where there is quarreling and open anger, pride is at work—and both parties are usually guilty.

As a young Christian, I recall how the powerful lure to sexual misbehavior was frequently dispelled in my thinking by the sudden recollection of that word in Ephesians where Paul says, "Let no one deceive you with empty words, for because of such things God's wrath comes on those who are disobedient. Therefore do not be partners with them" (Ephesians 5:6–7). That arrested me when I first heard it. Later, when I came to understand more fully what the wrath of God means—that it is not necessarily a lightning bolt from heaven or an auto accident or something like that, but rather it is the certain disintegration and brutalization of life, the natural consequences of sin in God's moral order—that verse took on even more power in my life.

A man once came to me for counseling. He was in the grip of a terrible emotional and spiritual depression—one of the most lonely, isolated, miserable people I have ever met—and we met together every week for over a year. His liberation began when he decided to pray a single phrase of Scripture whenever he was in the grip of his depression. It was the one portion of Scripture this man could, in faith, lay hold of. He rejected everything else I tried to point out to him. But one phrase stuck with him, and he prayed it again and again, the words of Jesus in the Garden of Gethsemane: "Not my will but Yours be done." At last, slowly, like the sun coming up, the light began to dawn, and you could see the change in his life. Today he is living a normal, free life. He was set free by "the sword of the Spirit," the *hrema*, the saying of God given specifically for his situation.

Obviously, the greater exposure there is to Scripture the more the Spirit can use this mighty sword in our lives. If you never read or study your Bible, you are terribly exposed to defeat and despair. You have no defense; you have nothing to put up against these forces that are at war with your soul. So I urge you to read your Bible regularly. Read all of Scripture, for each section has a special purpose.

The Christian who neglects the reading of the Scriptures is in direct disobedience to the will of the Lord. The Lord Jesus said, "You diligently study the Scriptures because you think that by them you possess eternal life. These are the Scriptures that testify about me" (John 5:39). That is the way you come to know Christ. There is no way apart from the Scriptures. And there is no way to come into full maturity as a Christian apart from the Scriptures.

What is the responsibility of the Christian when the Spirit places one of these sayings in your mind for some specific need in your life? What should you do when the Spirit places a sword in your hand? Take it! Wield it! Use it! Obey it! Do not reject it, neglect it, or treat it lightly. Take it seriously. The Spirit of God has brought it to mind for a purpose, so give heed to it and obey it.

## A balanced weapon

One final word of caution: We are also responsible to compare Scripture with Scripture. This is a very important matter. Remember, the devil can quote Scripture as well, as he did on one occasion with the Lord. But the quotations of Scripture by the devil are never balanced. The sword of the Spirit in the devil's hands is an uncouth weapon.

Remember how Jesus Himself gave us a great example of this when the devil came to tempt Him in the wilderness? The devil said to Him, "If you are the Son of God, tell these stones to become bread." Jesus immediately met him with the sword of the Spirit. He said, "It is written: 'Man does not live on bread alone, but on every word that comes from the mouth of God' " (Matthew 4:3–4).

Then the devil tried a new tactic. He came to Jesus and said, in effect, "Oh well, if you are going to quote Scripture, I can quote it, too. There is a verse in the Psalms, you know, which says that if you get yourself into a dangerous position, God will send his angels to uphold you." Taking Jesus to the top of the temple, the devil said, "Cast yourself from this height and all the crowd around will see and know that you are the Son of God." The Gospel account tells us: "Jesus answered him, 'It is also written: "Do not put the Lord your God to the test" ' " (Matthew 4:5–7).

Jesus knew how to handle the devil when the devil quoted Scripture. He said, "It is written again . . . It is written again . . . ." I urge you to take note of that. It is not enough to have someone quote a verse of Scripture to you or to have a verse come flashing into your mind. Ask yourself: Is this verse in balance with the rest of Scripture? Or has this verse been yanked out of context and twisted into saying something God never intended it to say?

Next, you remember, the devil showed Jesus all the kingdoms of the world. "All this I will give you," the devil promised, "if You bow down and worship me." And again our Lord answered him with the sword of the Spirit:

> Jesus said to him, "Away from me, Satan! For it is written: 'Worship the Lord your God, and serve him only.' "
>
> Then the devil left him, and angels came and attended him (Matthew 4:10–11).

The devil left him! That is always what happens. The devil is put to rout by the sword of the Spirit. It is this same sword Jesus so powerfully wielded that God has placed in your hands and mine!

Here then, is the Christian's complete armor: you in Christ and Christ in you; Christ, demonstrated as truth and experienced as righteousness and peace; and Christ, appropriated by faith and applied to life through the hope of salvation and the *hrema* sayings of God. That is all you need. If you are a Christian, you have the entire armor of God at your disposal.

On the other hand, if you are not a Christian there is no help for you. So the place to begin is to become a Christian. The Word of God has no comfort to give those who are not Christians; it has nothing to say to support or encourage someone who is not in Christ. The only way of escape from the lures, snares, and deceptions of the enemy is to receive Jesus Christ into your life. You must be delivered by the work of Jesus Christ from the kingdom of Satan into the kingdom of God. Then you can put on the armor of God.

So become familiar with this armor. Learn to use it, and call it to your defense when you are under attack. What good is armor if it rusts unused in a closet? No wonder Christians are constantly failing. Though they have the armor of God, they do not use it. So be a good soldier of the Lord; wear your armor and use it!

Remember: If you feel cold or lukewarm in your faith, you are under attack from the devil. If you find yourself depressed or discouraged; if you are bothered with doubts, fears, and anxieties; if you feel the lure of lusts, the crush of pain, or the numbness of disappointment—what must you do? Follow these steps—the belt of truth, the breastplate of righteousness, the preparation of the gospel of peace on your feet, the helmet of salvation, the shield of faith, and the sword of the Spirit. Think through these steps and systematically, deliberately, purposefully put on the full armor of God.

Do not give up if no immediate change occurs. Some-times, we must persevere in fighting spiritual battles and maintaining our defense against satanic attacks. We are brainwashed these days into expecting instant gratification, quick results, and immediate relief—but spiritual warfare cannot be waged in impatience. Remember, the attack may be prolonged and there are not always quick results. That is why the apostle Paul says, "After you have done everything . . . . [s]tand firm" (Ephesians 6:13–14). Victory is certain if you persevere.

The promise is sure: "Resist the devil, and he will flee from you" (James 4:7).

## Prayer

Father, I thank You for arming me and defending me against satanic attack. I thank You for giving me the means not only to be defended, but the means to take the offensive against the devil and send him running from me! Please bring your Word to mind in the times of need, pressure, discouragement, and defeat. Remind me to take your Word seriously and to apply this armor to me that You have given me in Jesus Christ. Lead me to the full, rich, exciting life that is mine as a Christian, living and battling evil in Your power and strength.

In the name of my Lord and Commander, Jesus the *Logos* of God, amen.

*And pray in the Spirit on all occasions with all kinds of prayers and requests. With this in mind, be alert and always keep on praying for all the saints.*

*Pray also for me, that whenever I open my mouth, words may be given me so that I will fearlessly make known the mystery of the gospel, for which I am an ambassador in chains. Pray that I may declare it fearlessly, as I should.*

**Ephesians 6:18–20**

# 9

# Facing the Onslaught

ONE NIGHT, JOHN PATON AND HIS WIFE—a missionary couple in the New Hebrides Islands—were awakened by chants outside their mission station. Looking out, they saw that scores of hostile islanders had surrounded the station with torches, intent on burning the place down and killing the missionary couple. The Patons got down on their knees and prayed throughout the night, asking God to deliver them. The tense, dark hours passed, yet the islanders kept their distance.

Finally, around daybreak, the Patons looked out the window—and the hostile tribesmen were gone. John Paton was baffled. There seemed to be nothing preventing the islanders from attacking, yet no attack came. Paton didn't find out why the islanders left so mysteriously until a year later, when the chief of the tribe was won to Christ.

Remembering the night-long siege of a year before, John Paton asked the newly converted chief why the tribesmen had departed instead of burning the mission station to the ground. "We were afraid of the men who were with you," the chief replied.

"What men?" asked Paton.

"There were a hundred tall men around the mission house that night," said the chief. "Their clothing shone with light, and they had swords in their hands. We knew that they would never let us harm you, so we went back to our village."

That is spiritual warfare at its most extreme! God does not always have to intervene in such a dramatic way on behalf of His children. Yet the battle is just as real, just as deadly, for you and me in our everyday lives as it was that night for the Patons in a mission station on the New Hebrides Islands. You and I are hemmed in by enemies every day, but God has provided a defense for us that will enable us to stand against the schemes and flaming arrows of the enemy. The apostle Paul has listed for us three steps we must take in order to "be strong in the Lord," and to resist the attacks of Satan:

Step 1: *Put on the armor of God.* Put on the *whole* armor—so that you may be able to stand against the schemes of the devil.

As we have seen, putting on the armor of God is far from being merely figurative—it is a practical step that you must take in order to defend yourself against the devil's attacks. It means remembering what Christ is to you and thinking through the implications of that relationship in terms of your present struggle and experience. Though putting on the armor of God is a very practical step, it is something we do in the realm of our thought-life. It is an adjustment of the attitude of your heart to reality, to things as they really are. It is the act of thinking through the implications of the facts revealed in God's Word.

Most of our problems in life stem from the fact that we do not see life as it really is. We suffer from illusions, from impaired vision, from limited perspective. This is why we desperately need to begin with the belt of truth—the revelation of the facts about life that we find in Scripture. Life is what God has declared it to be. When we face life on that realistic basis, we are able to live more effective, joyful, productive lives. We understand what is happening to us and why. We understand what is going on in the world and why. And we are able to arm ourselves for the battle that rages around us and within us—spiritual warfare. All this is part of putting on the full armor of God, of appropriating Christ and his strength so that we can live life realistically and effectively. We do all this in the realm of the thought-life.

When we are first learning to put on the full armor of God, it takes time and thought and attention. But like any other endeavor in life, we improve with practice. Eventually, putting on the full armor of God becomes a habit, it becomes natural. That, after all, is why soldiers train—to build soldierly habits, so that survival tactics, defensive tactics, and offensive tactics become second nature. In the heat of battle, a soldier does not want to have to think, "What do I do now? Where's my checklist? What did my sergeant tell me to do in this situation?" He wants to be able to act on instinct and carry out his training without hesitation.

So it is with soldiers of the Lord. When the devil presses his attack, we need to be ready to respond in a moment's notice, beginning with the belt of truth, and finishing with the sword of the Spirit. That kind of ready response comes only through continual practice, prayer, and awareness of the full armor of God on a daily basis.

Step 2: *Pray.* There is a very strong and powerful relationship between putting on the armor of God and prayer. These two steps belong together. It is not enough to put on the armor of God—you must also pray. It is not enough to pray—you must also have put on the armor of God. It is not a case of either/or. It's a case of both/and. Paul writes,

> And pray in the Spirit on all occasions with all kinds of prayers and requests. With this in mind, be alert and always keep on praying for all the saints.
>
> Pray also for me, that whenever I open my mouth, words may be given me so that I will fearlessly make known the mystery of the gospel, for which I am an ambassador in chains. Pray that I may declare it fearlessly, as I should (Ephesians 6:18–20).

Step 3: *Stand firm.* In the face of Satan's attacks, we are to stand firm in our faith with the certain knowledge that the battle is the Lord's. Our faith in His victory—a victory that is already accomplished on the cross—is what overcomes the world. In the next and final chapter, we will explore what it means, practically and biblically, to stand firm.

## The place to start

Notice that the apostle Paul in Ephesians 6 does not reverse the order of what we should do when we feel that attack of Satan. He does not instruct us to pray first, and then put on the armor of God. That is what we often try to do, and the result is a feeble, impotent prayer life. There is great practical help here if we carefully follow the designated order of Scripture.

I think most Christians, if they are honest, have to confess that they are dissatisfied with their prayer life. They feel it is inadequate and perhaps infrequent. All of us at times struggle to improve ourselves. Sometimes we struggle to improve the quality as well as the quantity of our prayer lives. Sometimes we adopt schedules that we attempt to maintain or we develop long lists of names and projects and places that we try to remember in prayer or we attempt to discipline ourselves in some way to a greater ministry in this realm. In other words, we begin with the doing, but when we do that, we are starting in the wrong place. We are violating our basic human nature in doing it that way. The place to start is not with the doing but with the thinking.

Now I am not suggesting that there is no place for Christian discipline. There is! I am not suggesting that we won't need to take our will and put it to the task and persevere in the hard work of prayer. There is a great need for that! But *first*, we should do what is involved in putting on the armor of God. *First*, think through the implications of faith, and *then* prayer will follow naturally and much more easily. It will be *thoughtful* prayer—prayer that has meaning and relevance.

Isn't that the problem with much of our praying? Our prayers are often so shallow and superficial. What is needed? Prayer should be an outgrowth of thoughtfulness about the implications of faith. That adds depth and significance to it. Prayer should be pointed and purposeful.

In Ephesians 6, Paul recognizes two categories of prayer, which he designates: (1) "all kinds of prayers" and (2) "requests." "All kinds of prayer," of course, is the widest classification; "requests" is the specific plea for help or provision made in prayer. And if you take the whole range of Bible teaching on this great subject of prayer, you will find that underlying all the biblical presentation of prayer is the idea that it is conversation with God. That is all it is; prayer is simply conversing with God.

## Family talk

When thinking about prayer, it is crucial to recall the position of a Christian—he is a member of the family of God. So prayer is not just a religious ritual—it is something much more real, much more profound: Prayer is *family talk*. It is a friendly, intimate, frank conversation with God. We have the privilege of such unrestricted communication with God by reason of the close and intimate relationship we have entered into with God by His grace, through faith in Jesus Christ. By faith in Christ, we pass out of the realm of strangerhood toward God and alienation from God; we have passed into the intimate family circle of the children of God. It is easy to talk within a family circle, and harm is done to family intimacy when family members maintain silence and refuse to talk.

So this is the essential nature of what Paul calls "all kinds of prayers." Prayer is nothing more nor less than family talk—a conversation with our Father.

What Paul calls "requests" are prayers of a somewhat special nature—but again, requests are also a form of family talk. The apostle James says, "You do not have, because you do not ask God" (James 4:2). In our conversation with God, it is perfectly proper to ask, because we are His children and He is our Father. Paul is saying, "After you have put on the armor of God—after you have thought through the implications of your faith—then talk to God about it." Tell Him the whole thing. Tell Him your reactions, tell Him how you feel, describe experiences and reactions to those experiences, and ask Him for what you need.

Prayer is often considered to be such a high and holy thing that it has to be carried on in some artificial language or resounding tone of voice. You hear this so frequently from the pulpit. Pastors adopt what has been aptly called a "stained-glass voice." They pray as though God were far off in some distant corner of the universe. I believe this sends a faulty message to people about what prayer truly is. It is important that we all understand that prayer is simply a conversation with our Father. It is what the apostle Paul describes so beautifully in his letter to the Philippians,

> Do not be anxious about anything, but in everything, by prayer and petition, with thanksgiving, present your requests to God. And the peace of God, which transcends all understanding, will guard your hearts and your minds in Christ Jesus (Philippians 4:6–7).

That is a wonderful study in prayer. Paul is saying that there are three simple steps involved in prayer:

(1) *Do not worry or be anxious.* Christian friend, do you hear what that says? Let go of your worries and anxieties—turn them over to the Lord! This is one of the major problems in Christian living today. Anxiety not only hinders our prayer life, but it also makes us ineffective soldiers for the Lord—and ineffective witnesses for the gospel. Christians become either stumbling blocks to nonChristians or a glowing testimony and witness to nonChristians depending on how they handle pressures and problems. A worried, anxious Christian gives the appearance that God cannot be trusted and the gospel provides no help in times of pressure and trials.

Since God is trustworthy, then Christians have nothing to worry about. He is in control. Since the gospel is true, Christians have nothing to be anxious about. All things ultimately work together for good in God's perfect plan. That is why Christians are continually exhorted in the Scripture not to worry. The more we worry, the less faith we demonstrate.

This is not to say that Christians should not be interested and concerned about life's problems, tragedies, and injustices. The Scriptures do not advocate a stoic, indifferent approach to life. We must be compassionate, concerned, and involved in life and the lives of people around us. We must care. But we demonstrate a lack of confidence in God whenever we are anxious, fretful, and worried.

Someone once said, "I'm so loaded down with worries that if one more thing goes wrong this week, it'll be two more weeks before I get around to worrying about it." Sometimes we make an artificial attempt to cure our worrying by sheer human will power. As one poet has humorously put it,

> I've joined the new 'Don't worry' Club
> And now I hold my breath;
> I'm so scared I'm going to worry
> That I'm worried half to death!

But Paul says, "Don't be anxious, don't worry about anything." How is that possible? It is only possible when you have put on the armor of God. Do not attempt it on any other basis. Worry comes from fear, and the only power that dissolves fear is recognizing the *facts*: the fact that God is in control; the fact that Jesus has already won the battle; the fact that we can trust the Lord to manage all events for our ultimate good and His ultimate plan—even tragedies, pain, and setbacks. When we put on the armor of God, we face the facts as they are. We accept reality as it truly is.

The next step Paul gives us for effective prayer is:

(2) *Pray about everything!* You may wonder, "Is God really interested in the little things as well as the big things?" Of course He is. He tells us so. The hairs on our heads are numbered by Him. God is concerned about everything, even the little things—so don't hesitate to bring Him any concern you have. God is a loving Father, and He is intimately concerned about every aspect of our lives.

The final step Paul gives us for effective prayer is this:

(3) *The result is peace.* Paul says that when we pray, "the peace of God, which transcends all understanding, will guard your hearts and your minds in Christ Jesus." That is the result of prayer, as Paul tells us in Philippians. The peace of God is a peace no one can understand or explain, a peace that comes to us despite our circumstances, and which does not arise out of emotions or events. It is supernatural in origin and nature. Can there be anything more relevant to the trouble and anxiety of this world than the peace of God?

## The essential link

Inherent in prayer are three basic facts:

(1) *When we pray, we recognize the existence of an invisible kingdom.* We would never pray at all if we did not have an awareness that Someone is listening, that behind what is visible there is an invisible kingdom. It is not far off in space somewhere; it is right here. It surrounds us on every side. We are constantly in touch with it even though we do not always realize it. It lies behind the façade of life, and all through the Scripture we are exhorted to take heed of this, to reckon with it and deal with it, to acknowledge that it exists.

(2) *We have confidence that the kingdom of God is highly significant and that it directly affects our lives.* Events in the visible realm are secretly motivated and driven by forces in the unseen realm. So—and here is a key point!—if you want to change the visibilities, you must start with the invisibilities. That is why prayer is so crucial. We are engaged in *spiritual warfare*. So we must conduct that

warfare in the spiritual realm, in the realm of God, in the realm of prayer.

(3) *Prayer is an essential part of bringing God's invisible power to bear on life in the visible realm.* The devil and his forces are fiercely dedicated to keeping human beings in the dark on this fact. The devil does not want you to know or believe that God truly does answer prayer. So it is crucial that we underscore this fact: Prayer is purposeful and powerful, because God is purposeful and powerful. God answers prayer.

The devil has been very effective in blunting and obliterating this truth from the minds of people today. We often hear such phrases as, "He doesn't have a prayer." Or, "There's nothing we can do now but pray." In other words, prayer is a last resort, a last ditch, a hopeless gesture, the last gasp when all other possibilities have been exhausted. Satan laughs whenever prayer is depicted in that way! He loves it when people think of prayer as a pitiful, pathetic, pointless gesture—and he hates it when people discover that prayer is direct access to the limitless power of the one who formed the planets and hurled the stars through space!

What an exhilarating thought: When we pray, God listens! When we make our requests, God acts! Prayer is an essential link to God's active involvement in the world today. Without prayer, God often does not work—He is a perfect Gentleman, and He does not go where He is not invited. But with prayer, He always works.

## Praying according to the promises

We must immediately add and underscore this biblical truth: *God answers prayer according to His promises.* There is a false concept of prayer held by many which suggests God answers any kind of prayer, no matter what you want or how you ask for it. This false teaching results in bitter disappointments and gives rise to the widespread belief that prayer is ineffectual. But God answers every prayer that is based upon His promises.

Prayer does not start with us; it starts with God. God must say He will do something before we are free to ask Him to do it. If God were to say yes to all of our demands, He would not be God. He would be our slave, a mere genie in a bottle. Instead of answering our prayers, He would be granting our wishes. That is neither a biblical nor a truthful description of how God works at all.

The God of the Bible is both the sovereign Creator and Lord of the universe, and He is a loving Father, and that is how we must approach Him. We should not presume to boss around the Creator of the universe. And we should understand how a healthy father-child relationship works. No loving parent commits himself to giving his children anything they want or demand. Rather, a loving parent makes it clear that he will do certain things for his children and not do other things. Within the scope of these parental promises and limits, a loving parent will commit himself to answer his children's requests.

For example, a loving parent may say, "I will grant your request for wholesome, nutritional snacks after school, but I will not grant your request for ice cream sundaes five times a day—I love you too much to grant a request that would harm your health." So it is with God. He has given promises, and they form the only proper basis for answered prayer. You and I may think that the request we have made of God is perfectly reasonable. We may imagine that if He were truly loving He would grant us the success, or healing, or blessing we ask for. But God sees more clearly than we do, and God may see (as He did when Paul prayed to be healed of a physical ailment, a "thorn in the flesh") that even something as seemingly beneficial as a physical healing may not be God's best for our lives.

This is what Paul means when he reminds us, "And pray in the Spirit on all occasions with all kinds of prayers and requests." What does that mean to "pray in the Spirit"? This is an area of great misunderstanding. Many take this phrase to describe the *emotions* we should have when we pray. They think it is necessary to be greatly moved before prayer can be effectual, that we should pray with great emotionalism. Of course, God is involved with us on an emotional level, and deep feelings are often a part of a vital prayer life. But emotionalism is not necessary to effective prayer, nor is emotionalism what Paul means when he urges us to "pray in the Spirit."

Quite simply, what Paul means is this: To "pray in the Spirit" is to pray according to the promises the Spirit has given, and it is based on the character of God which the Spirit has made known. God has never promised to grant our wishes, demands, beggings, pleadings, or cravings. He has only promised to answer prayers that are prayed in the way that He has outlined for us in His promises. He answers such prayers invariably and without partiality. He is no respecter of persons and He shows no favoritism in the matter of prayer.

In the realm of our personal needs—those needs that call forth most of our prayers, such as the need for wisdom, or patience, or grace, or strength, or endurance—God's promises to answer immediately and abundantly. He always answers that type of prayer to the full extent of our need, and in precisely the time-frame we need it (which is not necessarily the same thing as the time-frame we want or expect!). Jesus has made this promise to us: "Ask and it will be given to you" (Luke 11:9).

The apostle Paul confronts us with the fact that we must take this matter of prayer seriously and learn what God has promised. In other words, master this subject as you would master any other course of study you undertake. Scientists have mastered various areas in the realm of science. Teachers have become proficient at the art of teaching. Artisans give time and study to their trade. In the same way, we must learn to master the art of prayer. Though prayer is the simplest thing in the world—merely a conversation with God—it can also become the deepest and most profound experience in your life. As you grow in the practice and experience of prayer, you'll find that God is utterly serious about prayer. Through this two-way communication between ourselves and God, He makes His omnipotence and omniscience available to limited human beings, to you and me, in terms of specific promises He has made to us.

When you learn to pray on that basis, you will discover that exciting and unexpected things are constantly happening, that there is a quiet but mighty power at work in your life—a power on which you can rely. And as you learn to pray in this way, you'll find that a tremendous weapon, a mighty power to influence your own life and the lives of others, is put at your disposal.

## Open their eyes, Lord

We are not alone in this battle—this spiritual conflict with the unseen forces of evil. No, there are others around us who are weaker and younger in Christ than we are, and there are still others who are stronger and more mature than we. All of us are in this mighty army of God, fighting this battle shoulder to shoulder and side by side.

We cannot put on the armor of God for another person, but we can pray for that other person. We can call in reinforcements when we find a Christian brother or sister engaged in a struggle greater than themselves. We can share with them about the full armor of God, and help them to understand how to think through the panoply of armor God has equipped us with. We can be aware of other people's problems and trials, and we can pray for them. We are to pray that God will embolden their hearts, strengthen their bodies, clear their minds, and open their eyes to the danger that swirls around them. We can pray that God will supply them with the specific help and insight they need for the trial they are undergoing.

Notice how Paul asks this for himself in this very passage. "Pray also for me," he writes, "that whenever I open my mouth, words may be given me so that I will fearlessly make known the mystery of the gospel, for which I am an ambassador in chains. Pray that I may declare it fearlessly, as I should" (Ephesians 6:19–20). Even this mighty apostle has a deep sense of his need for prayer!

You find another notable example of Paul's desire for prayer in the closing verses of Romans 15, where he asks the Christians to pray for three specific needs: physical safety when he visits Jerusalem; a sensitive, tactful spirit when he speaks to Christians there; and an ultimate opportunity to visit the city of Rome (see Romans 15:30–32). Let me underscore this: Paul makes three specific requests, and the record of Scripture is that every one of those requests was answered exactly as Paul asked.

In reading through the prayers of Paul, I find that he deals with many matters. But one theme recurs again and again throughout his prayers: a request that the understanding of his fellow Christians would be enlightened. He repeatedly asks that the eyes of their minds—their intelligence—might be opened. This repetition in the apostle's prayers indicates the importance of intelligently understanding life—distinguishing what is true from what is false, what is real from what is phony. It also illustrates the power of the devil to blind and confuse us and to make things look very different from the way they really are. So the repeated prayer of the apostle is, "Lord, open their eyes that their understanding may be enlightened, that their intelligence may be clarified, that they may see things as they are."

In the letter of James, the importance of praying for others is forcefully underlined: "My brothers, if one of you should wander from the truth and someone should bring him back, remember this: Whoever turns a sinner from the error of his way will save him from death and cover over a multitude of sins" (James 5:19–20). The prayer of another person can change the whole atmosphere of one person's life—oftentimes overnight.

One Christmas eve my family and I were in the Sierra Nevada mountains of California, in a little Gold Rush town called Twain Harte. When the sun went down, the landscape around us was dry and barren. A few brown leaves swirled down from the trees; it was a typically bleak winter landscape. But when we awoke the next morning it was transformed into a wonderland of beauty. Every harsh line was softened, every blot was covered. A five-inch snowfall had fallen during the night and the whole landscape was quietly and marvelously transformed into a fairyland of delight.

I have seen this same thing happen in the life of an individual with a stubborn, hardened, self-willed attitude toward the things of God and His invisible reality. I have seen that person's heart softened and changed by prayer alone, performed secretly in the prayer closet of a faithful Christian. No words needed to be spoken, and would never have been received, by the person with the hardened heart. Prayer alone—the mysterious link between a faithful believer and the limitless power of our awesome God— was all that was required to perform the transformation.

At times, such transformations can take place virtually overnight—but at other times it takes much longer. I know of people whose lives were changed only after some faithful prayer warrior persevered on his or her knees for decades! But the change does come. Time is a factor that God alone controls, and he never puts a time limit on his instruction concerning prayer. He calls us to be faithful and constant in this ministry of prayer, both for ourselves and for one another. When we learn to pray as God teaches us to pray, we release in our own lives and in the lives of others the immense resources of God. We invite God to reach down into our lives and our world, supplying His strength, His power, His wisdom, His insight to heal the hurts, resolve the problems of this life, and win the battles of this life.

## Prayer

Father, I know so little about this mighty ministry of prayer. Lord, teach me to pray. Forgive me for the way I have often looked at prayer as though it were unimportant, insignificant, an optional religious exercise, a last resort. Help me to see prayer as my vital lifeline to You and Your mighty power. Help me to see reality clearly, especially the reality of prayer. Thank You, Lord, that You are not only infinitely powerful, You are also intimately involved in my life. I stand amazed that the Creator-God of the universe is also my Father, and that You invite me to climb into Your lap and call you "Daddy." What grace You give me! What a privilege You offer me! What a wonderful and exhilarating gift it is to be able to converse with You.

In the name of Jesus, our great model of prayer, amen.

*Put on the full armor of God so that you can take your stand . . .*

**Ephesians 6:11**

# 10

# The Infallible Posture

THE GAME OF FOOTBALL is warfare with rules. Because it is a kind of controlled, organized warfare, the game of football serves in several ways as an analogy for spiritual warfare. It is a game in which the contestants must "put on the full armor," the helmet, pads, and shoes, which enable them to be well-defended against injury. It is a game in which you must have a clear mind, you must be aware of the game plan, and you must be in constant contact with your coach—and of course, the same is true of spiritual warfare. It is a game of both offense and defense, a game that requires character and stamina, a game of both team effort and individual effort, and a game that is played out in an arena, surrounded by spectators—and the same, of course, is true of spiritual warfare.

I have often been impressed, when watching a hard-fought football game, to see the defending team's response to an especially hard push by their opponent's offensive platoon. Sometimes the offense will drive the defense back against their own endzone, and you will see a gritty, down-and-dirty struggle—a battle sometimes characterized as "three yards and a cloud of dust." One of the most thrilling sights in football is a determined goal-line defense, where the defenders simply line up on the scrimmage line against the opposing team and refuse to budge. They make a stand. They refuse to yield their ground.

A successful goal-line stand is often the climactic turning point of a game. There is nothing that takes the starch out of a football team's offense like getting stopped cold for four consecutive downs at the opponent's one-yard line. When an offense is unable to score in that situation, the team that was on defense now goes on offense. Often there is such a shift in energy and momentum at that point that the team that once was backed against the goal line now charges relentlessly up the field to score and even win the game!

So in football, in life, and in spiritual warfare, it is crucial that we learn how to make a stand and refuse to yield our ground.

### Learning to stand

Our study of spiritual warfare now brings us to the admonition of Paul which permeates and punctuates this passage in Ephesians 6, and which forms the aim and thrust of the entire passage. That admonition consists of one word which Paul repeats four different times in a few verses. It is the word *stand*. Notice how (as I've underscored certain phrases) the word *stand* marks these verses:

Put on the full armor of God so that you can *take your stand* against the devil's schemes. . . . Therefore put on the full armor of God, so that when the day of evil comes, you may be able to *stand your ground*, and after you have done everything, *to stand. Stand firm* then . . . (Ephesians 6:11, 13–14).

Everything Paul says is focused on enabling us to *stand* under the onslaught of the devil. Why does Paul focus so much on standing? Isn't "standing" a rather passive posture in a time of war? Why doesn't Paul say, "And after you have done everything, to *fight?*" Why doesn't he employ a militaristic concept that sounds more positive, forceful, and aggressive? Why doesn't he suggest that we prepare ourselves to advance, to charge? Does God really expect us merely to *stand?*

We must take these words seriously, for after all, these are not just words that might be used in a children's game. They are commands given in a very serious battle—a life-and-death struggle against consummate evil in the world. I am convinced that the apostle Paul uses the word *stand* because it is the only proper word to use. It is the only word that describes the authentic attitude we must have to insure absolute victory.

As we look at this word more carefully, we can see that it touches on three aspects of the struggle of life. The use of this word *stand* reveals to us the intensity of the struggle in which we are involved. We are told to stand because there are times when that is all we can do. The most we can possibly hope to achieve at times is to simply stand, unmoved. There are times in battle when a soldier can do no more than to simply protect himself and hold his ground. That is what this word implies to us.

Paul has already spoken in this passage about evil days that come. Thank God, all of life does not consist of evil days, but evil days do come. These are days when circumstances simply stagger us, when we face some combination of events—some disheartening tragedy or circumstance—that almost knocks us off our feet, and we can do nothing else but determine to stand where we are.

There are times when doubts plague us. We are exposed to intellectual attacks, and it is all we can do to simply cling to any amount of faith at all. We sometimes find ourselves overwhelmed by circumstances, fears, and worries so great that we can scarcely keep our heads because of the pressure. There are times when indifference seems to sap our spiritual strength so that we lose all our vitality. It drains our motivation, our will to act, and we seem unable to make ourselves do the simplest things to maintain and live out our faith—we cannot do anything but wearily stand our ground and try to remain on our feet.

This is all part of the struggle. We feel disturbed when there seems to be no growth and advance in our Christian faith. Our ministry and our witness seems ineffective. All the challenge and keenness of our spiritual life is gone. What are we to do then? Paul says we are to surround ourselves with the belt of truth, put on the whole armor of God, pray—and having done all, we are to stand! Putting on the armor and praying will not necessarily change the circumstances. God will not always end the battle or remove us from the struggle—sometimes we just have to persevere and withstand the onslaught.

So we stand! We hold our ground! We refuse to yield! If we remain immovable, if we resist the onslaught and hold our ground, the devil will eventually flee from us. This is the message that is woven throughout these verses in Ephesians 6.

## Cycles of trouble

Throughout the Bible, we see warning after warning that the evil days will come more frequently as we draw nearer the time of our Lord's return. The Bible has always told us that there will be evil days, but sometimes we misread certain predictions. There is a passage in 1 Timothy, for instance, that refers to the latter times. "The Spirit clearly says that in later times some will abandon the faith and follow deceiving spirits and things taught by demons" (1 Timothy 4:1). We read that as though it were a prediction of the closing moments of the age. But "latter times" means the whole of the age from our Lord's first coming until His return. Paul is not talking about one particular time of trouble reserved for the last moment; he is talking about repetitive cycles of trouble that come again and again throughout the whole course of these latter days.

But the Word of God also suggests that these cycles become fiercer in intensity and more widespread in their impact as the age draws to its close. There is a growing awareness in our day that we live in a one-world community. We often hear talk about the "global community," the "global economy," the "global village." We are no longer separated from other peoples by great distances of thought, distance, or time. What happens on the other side of the world today affects us tomorrow. We are very much aware of this.

Evil days were once limited geographically. In the past, persecution grew intense in various places and economic pressures became severe in certain areas, while other parts of the world prospered. But now, as the present age continues, events in one small troubled region—Kuwait, Bosnia, Somalia, Haiti, Korea, Nicaragua, Israel—can have a planet-wide impact.

America today may seem to be an island of relative peace and security in a wide sea of trouble and distress—but that sea is constantly lapping at our shores, eroding our illusion of security. There is an irresistible, rising tide of trouble in the world. Regardless of any temporary time of prosperity, any technological progress, any brief respite from political or social upheaval, we must honestly admit that global conditions are not getting better in our world; they are worsening. Public and private morality is declining. Racial and social unrest is growing. Disrespect for law and justice, for standards of right and wrong, is growing. Hatred of Christians and persecution of the Christian faith are on the rise.

The solutions of many sincere people—educational solutions, scientific discoveries, economic improvements, legislative and governmental solutions—are not working. Such efforts have their place, of course, but do not solve the core problem of the human condition. The real problem lies beyond the reach of superficial, external fixes. It is embedded deep within the hearts and souls of human beings, who are in turn enmeshed within the cruel and repressive invisible power structure that dominates this planet—the world rulers of this present darkness. Only the delivering power of Jesus Christ is adequate to deal with these spiritual forces. Even nonChristians are coming to the conclusion that there are no human solutions to the problems that confront the human race at the threshold of the new millennium. As social critic Richard Wright observes in his book, *The Outsider*:

> I remind you of what is happening in the great cities of the earth today: Chicago, Detroit, Pittsburgh, London, Manchester, Paris, Tokyo, Hong Kong and the rest. These cities are for the most part vast pools of human misery, networks of raw human nerves exposed without benefit of illusion or hope to the new godless world wrought by industrial man. The people in these cities are lost. Some of them are so lost that they no longer even know it, and they are the real lost ones. They haunt the movies for distraction. They gamble. They depress their sensibilities with alcohol, or they seek strong sensations to dull their sense of a meaningless existence.

That is the world we now face, and because of it there are many who falter in their faith. All too often we read in the newspapers of outstanding Christian leaders who have suffered moral collapse and have been laid on the shelf, their ministry and their testimony brought to an end. This is happening everywhere.

## To reveal the false

Why does God permit such a monstrous rise of evil in the world? It is no mystery. He tells us in His Word: He permits it in order to separate the phony from the true. In Hebrews 12:26–29, we are told that everything that *can* be shaken *will* be shaken. God is allowing these testings to reveal the genuine and to remove what can be shaken in order that what cannot be shaken might remain for all to see:

> At that time his voice shook the earth, but now he has promised, "Once more I will shake not only the earth but also the heavens." The words "once more" indicate the removing of what can be shaken—that is, created things—so that what cannot be shaken may remain. Therefore, since we are receiving a kingdom that cannot be shaken, let us be thankful, and so worship God acceptably with reverence and awe, for our "God is a consuming fire."

So evil days come. Indeed, they are coming. They are upon us. When they come into your own personal experience, remember that the word of God to you is to put on the whole armor of God, to pray, and to stand. Perhaps you will realize that there is nothing else you can do, but you can win if you will stand.

I once received a prayer letter from a missionary in the jungles of New Guinea. In that letter, this faithful Christian servant caught the very spirit of our Christian faith in these words:

> Man, it is great to be in the thick of the fight, to draw the old devil's heaviest guns, to have him at you with depression and discouragement, slander, disease. He

doesn't waste time on a lukewarm bunch. He hits good and hard when a fellow is hitting him. You can always measure the weight of your blow by the one you get back.

When you're on your back with fever and at your last ounce of strength, when some of your converts backslide, when you learn that your most promising inquirers are only fooling, when your mail gets held up, and some don't bother to answer your letters, is that the time to put on mourning? No, sir. That's the time to pull out the stops and shout, Hallelujah!

The old fellow's getting it in the neck and hitting back. Heaven is leaning over the battlements and watching. "Will he stick with it?" And as they see Who is with us, as they see the unlimited reserves, the boundless resources, as they see the impossibility of failure, how disgusted and sad they must be when we run away.

Glory to God! We're not going to run away. We're going to stand.

*Stand!* That is the word of the dedicated, authentic soldier of the Lord!

## A defensive battle

Now there is a second truth indicated by this word *stand*. It indicates to us the character of the battle the Christian faces. The act of standing implies primarily a defensive action, and the message of Paul in Ephesians 6 is that a strong defense will win the day. I know that this runs counter to the conventional wisdom that "the best defense is a good offense." But if a castle is under attack from an army, the battle is not won by those in the castle venturing forth to overwhelm the army outside. The battle is won by remaining secure within the walls and repelling all invasion. This is a picture of our Christian life. Ours is a defensive battle. We are not out to take new ground; we are to defend that which is already ours.

In the Christian battle the offensive work was accomplished some 2,000 years ago upon the cross and in the resurrection. The Lord Jesus is the only one who has the power to take the offense in this great battle with the prince of darkness—and he has already done that. All that we need as soldiers of the cross is what has already been given to us. We do not have to fight for it. We do not battle to be saved, or fight to be justified, or struggle to be forgiven, or wrestle to be accepted into the family of God. All these things are given to us already. They were won by Another who, in the words of Paul in Colossians, "disarmed the powers and authorities, [and] made a public spectacle of them, triumphing over them by the cross" (Colossians 2:15).

So Jesus has already won the battle, launching His offensive from a rugged wooden cross. Now it is up to us to stand the ground that He has gained on our behalf, to use the armor He has given us, to fully enjoy and experience the new life and the grand adventure that is ours. The enemy fights to keep us ignorant of the resources we have, so that we will not use those resources to the full. That is where the battle lines are.

We do not need to take new ground as Christians. In fact, we cannot do so. The full victory has already been accomplished and given to us. As Jude says, near the very end of the New Testament, "I . . . urge you to contend for the faith that was once for all entrusted to the saints" (Jude 3). We are to hold on to that which God gives us and not let any of it be lost or taken from us. That is what "contend for the faith" means. It does not mean to attack everyone who does not agree with you. It means to hold on to what God has already given you and utilize it to the full. Paul writes with the same idea in mind to the Corinthians, "Be on your guard; stand firm in the faith; be men of courage; be strong" (1 Corinthians 16:13). Do not surrender an inch of ground even though others do.

"But this sounds so negative!" you might say. "I don't want to be on the defensive! I want to take the offensive against evil! This sounds as if Christians are to dig a foxhole, jump in it, and wait for the enemy to come storming in! It almost sounds as if Christians are to cover their heads and retreat from the world—as if we are trying to get through life and on to heaven without becoming contaminated by the world! I don't want to view my role in the world in such a negative way!" That, of course, is a misinterpretation of what the Bible means when it says we are "to stand." Yes, this does refer to a defensive action—but the amazing thing is that this kind of defensive action becomes the greatest offense the Christian can mount.

The fact is, the Christian who learns to stand, clad in the full armor of God, energized and empowered by prayer, his feet planted and immovable, is the only one who can truly affect the world. He is the only one who will reflect the love of Christ in the midst of unlovely situations. He is the only one who will be able to manifest peace and serenity, poise and assurance in the midst of a troubled and unhappy world.

Christians who learn to stand make the world as livable and marginally decent as it is. We Christians are the salt of the earth, Jesus said. Salt is a preservative; Christians are the preservative of society—we are all that stands in the way of ultimate corruption and social decay. But if we, the salt, have lost our savor, what good are we? We are good for nothing but to be thrown out and trampled under the feet of men! That is, by and large, what the world is doing with the Christian church these days—treading it underfoot as worthless, useless. That is because we have not learned to stand—and thus we have lost our saltiness, our ability to help preserve our society against corruption.

But when a Christian truly learns to become the kind of salt God intended him to be, when we learn to stand while the world around us is falling, people are amazed. They demand to know our secret. They long to know what enables us to stand in a falling-down world. "What do these people have?" they wonder. "They don't give way like we do; they don't go along with the rest of crowd. They resist pressure and temptation, and they stand for something larger than themselves."

That is true manhood in Christ, true womanhood in Christ. That is what God is after in our lives. That is what He wants to make us in Christ. But the purpose of the battle is not to become that kind of a person, for that is precisely the kind of person Christ makes us when we follow Him. The battle is to show it, to reveal it, to manifest what we are. So put on the whole armor of God—all that Christ is! Then pray! Then, having done all, stand your ground!

## The fatal flaw

Now there is a third truth indicated by this word *stand*, and that is the certainty of victory. If putting on the armor of God and prayer makes it possible to stand unmoved and immovable, then there is nothing more required to win. After all, if a castle cannot be taken, the attacking army has nothing left to do but to withdraw. They are defeated.

Throughout this book, we have talked about the cleverness of Satan, his subtlety of attack, his schemes, and the impossibility of defeating him by human wisdom. Every saint in the record of Scripture, every believer throughout history, has been, at one time or another, defeated by the devil when he tried to match wits with the devil in his own strength. This is true. But it is also true that when any saint, any believer, even the newest and the weakest, stands in the strength of Christ, puts on the whole armor of God, and prays, the devil is always defeated.

This is because of a fatal flaw in the devil's approach. When the believer stands on the ground of faith, the devil always over-reaches himself. Satan goes too far. That is because he commits himself to extremes, and in that lies his defeat. Sooner or later, the truth of reality must become apparent. The devil can never take the ground of truth because that, of course, would defeat his own aims. God is truth, and the devil cannot defend and support God, for he is out to attack and outwit God. All the devil can do is take the ground of untruth, extremism, distortion, and deception. Ultimately, because God is truth (and truth is always the reflection of God), truth must finally prevail. Because God never changes, this has been true throughout the entire history of the world, and it will be the continuing record on into eternity.

Abraham Lincoln expressed it well in that famous quotation: "You can fool some of the people all of the time, and you can fool all of the people some of the time, but you can't fool all of the people all of the time." Truth comes out. God is truth. If we live with truth long enough, stand on it long enough, it will prevail and reveal itself.

This explains what we have referred to at times as the phenomenon of "fashions in evil." Anyone who has been a Christian for any length of time learns that error comes in cycles, like clothing styles. You may be out of style for awhile, but if you stay with the same style long enough, it will come back in. If you are standing on the truth of God, there will be times when it is regarded with utter scorn by the world. The truth will be laughed at and you will be mocked. But if you follow those foolish people who think they must adjust to every sweeping current of the times and try to maintain what they call "intellectual respectability" at all times, you will find that as fast as you adjust, styles change and you are out of style again.

But if you continue to stand fast on what God has declared unchangeable, you will find a strange phenomenon happening: The very truths that were attacked by the world a decade ago will become fashionable again, and hailed as the newest discovery of the brilliant intellect of men. Then you, who have believed it all along, are right back in style again. Truth never changes.

The devil will ultimately be defeated if you simply stand on what God has said. It is his inevitable fate to be defeated by the very weapons he tries to use against God and his people. That is why it is so foolish to believe the lies of the devil.

The devil is much like the villains in the old melodramas. Remember how the plot always develops? The heroine appears to be doomed, and the villain has the upper hand. He twirls his mustache and rubs his hands with glee. But at the critical moment, the hero arrives and everything changes. The villain is beat by his own devices, and he slinks off the stage muttering, "Curses! Foiled again!" That is the devil's fate when he attacks any Christian who is willing to make a stand and hold his ground without yielding.

When we are tempted to yield our ground, we should look to the cross. Remember, the cross was not always the symbol of victory over sin and death. At that awful moment in time when Jesus was nailed to those rough wooden beams and raised against a dark sky, the cross looked like the supreme achievement of the devil. All the powers of darkness howled with triumph as they saw the Son of God beaten and wounded, rejected and despised, nailed to a death-gallows. Jesus Himself said, "But this is your hour, when darkness reigns" (Luke 22:53).

Yet that was the very moment when the devil was defeated!

In the cross, all that Satan had risked was destroyed, and the devil and his angels were disarmed by the power of Jesus Christ. This is what God does all through life. Yes, the devil still works his horrible mischief in the world. He still sends sickness, darkness, and suffering. It is all the work of Satan. But that is not the end of the story. God takes all the misery and horror that Satan inflicts, and He uses it in our lives to strengthen us, to bless us, to teach us, to enlarge us, and to give us a vibrant ministry in the world.

Whatever our battles and skirmishes with the devil, whatever wounds we may suffer in this good and noble fight, God gives us the ultimate victory. That is our ultimate assurance. That is the whole of the story.

## The final issue

Here is a statement from a Christian man who has been an invalid all his life—one of those lonely, obscure people who live in constant pain, who does not know what it means to be able to use his physical body in any way except in pain and suffering. But he writes this:

> Loneliness is not a thing of itself, not an evil sent to rob us of the joys of life. Loneliness, loss, pain, sorrow—these are disciplines, God's gifts to drive us to His very heart, to increase our capacity for Him, to sharpen our sensitivities and understanding, to temper our spiritual lives so that they may become channels of His mercy to others and so bear fruit for His kingdom. But these disciplines must be seized upon and used, not thwarted.
>
> Trials must not be seen as excuses for living in the shadow of half-lives, but as messengers, however painful, to bring our souls into vital contact with the Living God, that our lives may he filled to overflowing with Himself in ways that may, perhaps, be impossible to those who know less of life's darkness.

That is what it means to stand. One of these days, the Bible says, the struggle will end. It will end for all of us at the end of our lives, but it may end before that in the coming of the Lord. Some day the struggle will be over; there is no doubt of that. And some day it will be written of some, as it is recorded in the book of Revelation, "They overcame [the devil] by the blood of the Lamb and by the word of their testimony; they did not love their lives so much as to shrink from death" (Revelation 12:11).

The great issue of life is not how much money we make or how much status we acquire or whether we achieve that corner office or how much of a name we make for ourselves. The great issue, above all, is whether it can be written of us, as we come to the end of this struggle, that we overcame by the blood of the Lamb and by the word of our testimony, for we did not love our lives unto death.

As the world grows darker, the truth of Jesus Christ burns brighter. And the brightest truth of all is this: He has already won the war in which we fight. The war was over the moment He shouted, "It is finished!"

We do not have to march against the devil. We do not have to charge against the enemy. We merely have to assume the unassailable, invincible, infallible posture. As the days grow darker and more evil, *we will not be moved*! We have put on the armor of God, we have planted our feet. Though the enemy is attacking, we are not afraid, for the battle has already been won.

Stand firm, my friend! Stand your ground! Ours is the victory in Christ!

## Prayer

Lord, I live in perilous times, but I thank You that I do not get my view of life from the newspapers, nor from the television screen, but from Your living Word—the only reliable window on reality and truth. Help me to believe it and obey it. Above all, help me to stand, undefeated and invincible in Christ.

In the name of Jesus, who has already won the battle upon the cross, and who exploded from the tomb in glorious resurrection power, to Him be all the honor, all the praise, and all the victory, amen!

## Note to the Reader

The publisher invites you to share your response to the message of this book by writing Discovery House Publishers, Box 3566, Grand Rapids, MI 49501, USA. For information about other Discovery House books, music, or videos, contact us at the same address or call 1-800-653-8333. Find us on the Internet at http://www.dhp.org/ or send e-mail to books@dhp.org.